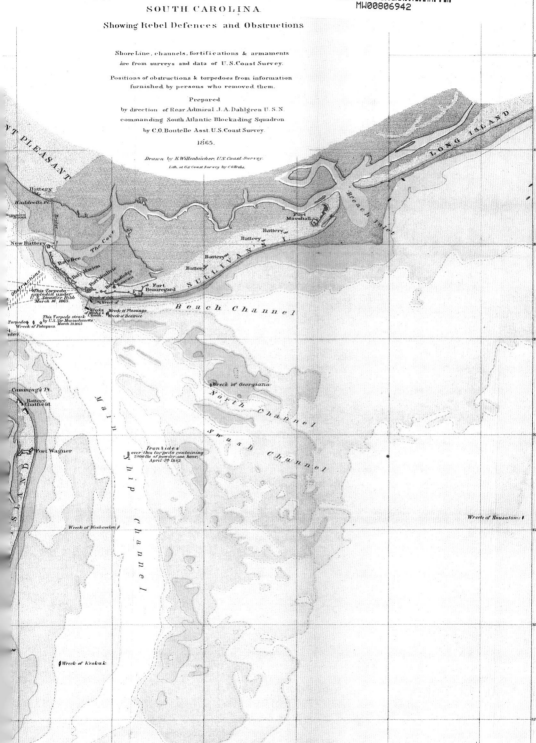

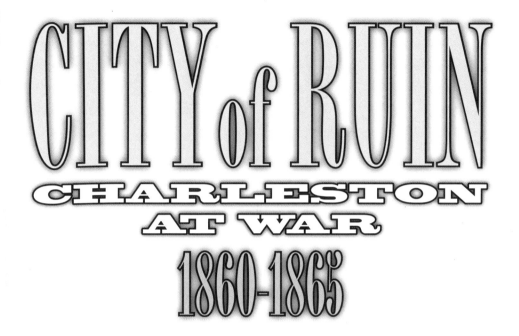

CITY of RUIN

CHARLESTON AT WAR

1860-1865

BRIAN HICKS

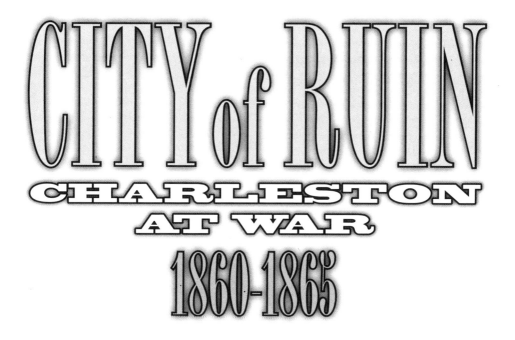

CITY of RUIN

CHARLESTON AT WAR

1860-1865

BRIAN HICKS

EVENINGPOSTBOOKS
Our Accent is Southern!
www.EveningPostBooks.com

Published by
Evening Post Books
Charleston, South Carolina

Editors: John M. Burbage and Rick Nelson
Designer: Gill Guerry

First printing 2012
Printed in the United States of America

A CIP catalog record for this book has been applied
for from the Library of Congress.

ISBN: 978-0-9825154-5-7

DEDICATION

For Nate,
A Native
Charlestonian

TABLE OF CONTENTS

INTRODUCTION

WHERE IT ALL BEGAN

A round Charleston, most people just call it "The War."

It's shorthand, a contraction, a reference to something so familiar – so ingrained in local culture – that there's no need to ask which war. Only one matters in this town. Other local titles for the American Civil War include: "The War Between the States," "The War of Northern Aggression" or, the one that truly captures the Charleston attitude, "Our Late Unpleasantness." But, bottom line, all one really has to say is The War and people around here catch on fast.

No other city is so inextricably linked to our nation's defining drama. The seeds of secession took root in Charleston, the first overt acts of war occurred here and the first shots were fired at Fort Sumter in a conflict that would eventually lead to the deaths of at least 620,000 Americans. Between the spring of 1860 and the spring of 1861 the nation was fixated on the events transpiring in this city; nothing less than the fate of an entire country depended on what happened in Charleston. And a lot was happening.

Today, many locals know the general order of events: South Carolina's secession vote was cast in Charleston; federal troops abandoned Fort Moultrie and occupied the unfinished Fort Sumter; Southern troops fired on the supply ship *Star of the West;* and, eventually, the Confederates bombarded Fort Sumter in the first battle of the Civil War. But despite their familiarity with the basic story, few people know the details behind the chain of events that led the United States down the road to disunion and, ultimately, war. Of course, some still even disagree over why the Civil War was ever fought in the first place.

Historians have long claimed that an average of one book has been published about the Civil War each day since the conflict ended. That statistic – probably apocryphal – was little comfort when *The Post and Courier* began planning its coverage for the 150th anniversary of the American Civil War.

Newspapers love anniversaries. They offer a chance to reflect, retell amazing stories or even make new points about events that shaped their community. And no event shaped Charleston like The War. *The Post and Courier* – the South's oldest daily newspaper – had to do something special to mark this defining era in the city's history. The question was: Is there anything new to say?

Standard newspaper *modus operandi* would be to interview a chorus line of historians and academics and publish stories focused on their thoughts about what the war means today, to dissect the national attitude 150 years after these events. But that seemed anti-climactic, dull and not nearly big enough to commemorate the city's integral role in the Civil War. It is Charleston's epic conflict, and it deserves epic treatment.

In the 1960s, Arthur Wilcox and Warren Ripley did a series of stories for *The News and Courier* that was ultimately collected in the booklet "The Civil War at Charleston." Over the years that collection proved immensely popular and it still remains a local classic. Taken as a whole, their stories ably recount all that happened in the city between 1860 and 1865. In early 2010, *Post and Courier* Content Editor Rick Nelson and I were approached about using the Wilcox and Ripley stories as the basis of a 20-part series on the war. As you might expect, both of us were apprehensive about tampering with a classic – the journalistic equivalent of playing a cover tune. We wanted to find a new way to tell the story, our own way. That wasn't going to be easy, given the aforementioned statistic.

The answer came to us, like many bolts of inspiration, from the most obvious place: newspapers. One of the most famous papers of the era was the *Charleston Mercury* "Extra" edition from Dec. 20, 1860 – the broadsheet that announced South Carolina's secession with the bold headline "The Union is Dissolved!" This was as good a starting point as any. I knew a bit about *Mercury* owner Robert Barnwell Rhett and his pro-secession newspaper from earlier wanderings through history, but had never really read much of the *Mercury*. When I did, using microfilm in *The Post and Courier* library, I found the story of this city's role in the war laid out in black and white. While the *Daily Courier* (*The Post and Courier's* direct ancestor) covered the events leading up to and during the war with the comprehensive nature expected of the city's newspaper of record, the *Mercury* filled the nooks and crannies with a personality that was undeniably Charleston.

Despite their obvious political slant, Rhett and his son – *Mercury* editor R.B. Rhett Jr., whose voice fills these pages – related the war as everyday Charlestonians experienced it, from the parades in the streets to the daily bombardment that eventually forced many to flee their homes. They chronicled local events only tangentially related to the war, but which give the story additional texture. The *Mercury* recorded the ever-changing mood of people living in a war zone.

The Rhetts inadvertently also painted a vivid portrait of how slaves and free blacks lived in Charleston at the time – one of the lesser-explored aspects of the city's wartime history. In many retellings of the conflict, Charleston is portrayed as a one-dimensional town full of fire-eaters and slave owners; the truth is a lot more complex, nuanced and multi-layered. In that respect, the city is a microcosm of the entire war.

This book is based on the 20-part series that came out of a year of research and writing and that ran in *The Post and Courier* on Sundays from December 2010 through April 2011. The pieces tell the story of the Holy City from 1860 through its fall in the winter of 1865, with a coda a year into Reconstruction.

However, this book goes beyond that series. As the stories ran in the newspaper, we were contacted by people who offered additional anecdotes or supplied new information that never appeared in the pages of the *Mercury*. For instance, after the story about the fire that decimated the city in December 1861 was published, Harlan Greene at the College of Charleston informed us the college had a paper written by the fire chief from that time period, notes which included even more information about the disaster. So many tidbits came in over those five months – and so much of what happened had to be truncated to fit the series into the paper – that we decided to expand the story.

In *City of Ruin* we hear more from Abner Doubleday, the Union soldier who fired the first shot from Fort Sumter; famed Confederate diarist Mary Chesnut; and even James Louis Petigru, the former state attorney general who had resisted South Carolina's secession movement a generation earlier. Petigru tangled with Rhett himself during the nullification crisis, a precursor to the war. And of course, there is even more reportage from the Rhetts and the *Mercury* in these pages. In all, this book is half-again as long as the newspaper series that spawned it and offers an even broader perspective of Charleston during the war.

There is an old saying that newspapers are the first draft of history. That's true, but often some of the most telling stories never survive beyond that initial draft. It is fortunate that 150 years after the fact those old papers can still offer a fresh perspective and provide a new way to tell an old story. This is not simply an ode to old times not forgotten, it is the epic story of one city's important role in this country's defining moment.

Brian Hicks
Charleston, South Carolina
July 5, 2011

Reception of the news of the election of Mr. Lincoln, City Hall, Charleston.

CHAPTER 1

MERCURY RISING

There was great excitement on Broad Street that evening.

Local men dressed in fine suits congregated on Charleston's busiest thoroughfare, their voices carrying along the dirt street, their shadows dancing on the walls of three-story storefronts, most of which had been closed for hours. It was Nov. 6, 1860, and the enthusiastic gentlemen of the Holy City had gathered in front of the telegraph offices and the headquarters of the Charleston *Mercury* to await news of the nation's presidential election.

Years of strife and decades of conflict had all come down to one vote. Nothing less than the future of the country rested on the electorate's decision. Although the mood outside the newspaper office was festive, there was a palpable anxiety running through Charleston. For decades, the South — and South Carolina in particular — had grown increasingly restless with the state of the Union. In 1832 the state nearly brought the country to war over tariffs that its politicians considered unfair. Two decades later the Legislature declared that South Carolina had the right to secede, although lawmakers stopped short of following through on the threat.

These politicians claimed that the federal government was growing too powerful, infringing on the rights of states to control their own destinies. Much of this was a response to limitations that Congress had put on slavery and the actions of Northern states, which often refused to return fugitive slaves to their owners. To Southern politicians of the day, this was largely an issue of economics. While the North was marching into the Industrial Age, the South clung to an agrarian economy, one that was

Illinois politician Abraham Lincoln became the wedge in the nation's growing divide.

almost wholly dependent on slave labor. The men who controlled South Carolina believed the federal government wanted to put that most "peculiar institution" out of business.

And that would cripple the South's economy.

The intricacies of the situation eluded most Southerners. They knew only what they were told by firebrand politicians: The sectional strife was an issue of states' rights and that the North was trying to establish a permanent subjugation of the South. They said this plot was manifested in the creation, six years earlier, of the Republican Party – a political organization built by former Whigs and, most tellingly, anti-slavery activists.

And now, one of these "Black Republicans" – as Southerners derisively called members of the party – stood a good chance of becoming president.

He was a country lawyer from Illinois named Abraham Lincoln. This tall, lanky man had become something of a sensation in the North and western reaches of the country, drawing huge crowds on the rare occasion he could be coaxed into public. Despite a thin political resume, with only a few years in the state Legislature and a single term in the U.S. House of Representatives, Lincoln was the favorite to win the presidency.

Abraham Lincoln had come to personify the villainy of the North, the symbol of what Southerners considered wrong with the country. This was largely based on criticisms of slavery he had made several years earlier during an unsuccessful Senate campaign. Now, his political fortunes appeared to be much better. For a year South Carolina politicians had claimed that if Lincoln was elected, the state would have no choice but to secede. Southern leaders had promoted Kentuckian John Breckinridge for the presidency, promising the Union would remain intact if he were elected. They likely offered such bold pronouncements with their minds made up: Breckinridge was the longest of long shots, the nominee only of Southern Democrats.

All of this consternation culminated on election night in Charleston.

The men awaited the results of the presidential election in the shadow of the city's Revolutionary past. The *Mercury* office stood at the east end of Broad Street, not far from the Exchange Building on Bay Street, which housed the city's Post Office. The men likely passed the time regaling each other with stories, jokes or predictions of the election's outcome – idle talk that belied the weight of the evening's outcome. Soon, the results began to arrive via telegraph.

The first dispatch came from Connecticut. The telegraph office reported that the state had gone for Lincoln by a majority of several thousand votes. Not long after that, the telegraph operator received word that North Carolina had chosen Breckinridge – the sectional split proceeding as predicted.

It was the third dispatch that finally stirred the crowd into a sustained frenzy. The Associated Press sent out a bulletin that declared, according to the *Mercury*, "Lincoln's election was certain, and that trifling details were unnecessary."

The reaction of the men on Broad Street might have seemed odd at first. The *Mercury* reported that after they read the Associated Press story, "a long and continued cheering" went up. This was not, the paper felt compelled to clarify, a celebration of Lincoln, but for "a Southern Confederacy."

"The greatest excitement prevailed, and the news spread with lightning rapidity over the city," the *Mercury* reported.

Robert Barnwell Rhett had anticipated this moment for decades.

A lifelong politician, Rhett served as South Carolina's attorney general, a state legislator and a member of Congress, both in the House and the Senate. For much of that time, he was one of the country's most extreme proponents of secession. His position was so strident that it long ago caused him to break with his political mentor, John C. Calhoun. The late Calhoun – former vice president and the father of South Carolina politics – was an outspoken proponent of nullification, limited government and slavery. But the old man was not willing to go far enough on secession to suit Rhett. For him, it was an obsession.

Rhett was born in 1800 as Robert Barnwell Smith. The Beaufort native changed his name in 1837 – an act he claimed was done simply to honor his ancestor, William Rhett. But William C. Davis, his biographer, would later note that Barnwell Smith knew full well the political and social benefit of a "more distinctive and distinguished" surname. In South Carolina, a politician needed every advantage he could get.

The issues of the day shaped his political platform. Rhett served in the state Legislature between 1826 and 1832, when the federal government first raised the ire of South Carolinians. State politicians were enraged over an 1828 tariff that taxed British imports so heavily that the English demand for Southern cotton dropped considerably. This "Tariff of Abominations," as the politicians called it, was a damning blow to the South Carolina economy.

Although the rates were moderated with a new tariff in 1832, the state called a convention to approve the nullification of any federal laws with which it disagreed, and the future Barnwell Rhett became one of its most vocal proponents. This precursor to civil war ended only after President Andrew Jackson threatened military action against the state, and Henry Clay – then a United States senator – negotiated a compromise to gradually lower the tariff even more. The crisis was averted, but the seeds of rebellion were sown.

Rhett found a new platform from which to expound on his states' rights belief as South Carolina's attorney general. In 1834 a court case concerning a "test oath" found its way into the state Court of Appeals. South Carolina's nullification ordinance, passed during the earlier crisis, contained a provision that required civil and military officers to swear allegiance to the state (presumably over the nation). When one man refused to take the oath, his application to a state militia was refused. Another military officer lost his commission when he declined to take the oath. Between these two cases, a lawsuit was born.

Rhett (still Smith at the time) argued in favor of the oath on behalf of the state against the plaintiffs' attorney, James Louis Petrigru – a well-known and respected politician, as well as Smith's former professor. In the proceedings Rhett claimed that the U.S. Constitution and the Congress were creations of the states and held no sovereignty – only the states did. His fiery rhetoric ultimately lost to Petrigru's Unionist position, but the man who would soon call himself Barnwell Rhett was only beginning to hone his states' rights message.

He would continue to strengthen his argument over the following two decades.

Rhett so zealously promoted his idea of a separate Southern nation that he — like other secessionists, such as Virginian Edmund Ruffin — had been dubbed a "fire-eater" by Northerners. He once had tried to stir sentiment for secession at a convention of Southern states in Nashville. When he failed, Rhett receded from public view somewhat. For a long time, most politicians distanced themselves from his rhetoric.

In the decade since his appearance in Nashville, he continued to push his views in the Charleston *Mercury*, an unabashed pro-secession publication. The newspaper's unflagging support for Rhett over the years had long caused people to speculate that he was actually its owner (his brother-in-law was, in fact, its long-time editor). In 1857 Rhett surprised no one when he purchased the new paper and named his son, Robert Barnwell Rhett Jr. as its editor. From that point on, there was no stopping the secessionist's message.

After years in the political desert, Rhett's views soon became fashionable again, helped in part by national news that chronicled the growing tension between North and South. Rhett became a local hero of the Southern movement. Earlier that fall, he was honored with a life-size transparency of himself in the window of the Charleston Restaurant. The city even named its new militia the Rhett Guard. As Davis later wrote, Rhett "could hardly help being immensely satisfied with all these expressions that he had been right all along and that at last South Carolina had caught up to him."

Of course, by the late 1850s, the long discourses on secession published in the *Mercury* were largely preaching to the choir. No place in the United States was more ripe for revolution than South Carolina, and Charleston in particular.

Charleston had become a world left behind by much of the country. In 1800 it was the fifth-largest city in the country — a city nearly the equal of New York or Philadelphia. But times were changing and, as the decades of the 19th century began melting away, Charleston's standing — and population — failed to keep pace. By 1860 Charleston's influence was on the wane. *Harper's Weekly* declared that one of the oldest cities in the country was "once one of the greatest cities on this continent."

Once.

Part of the reason for this seemed to be the state's political leaders and their fierce devotion to the agrarian economy, an economy fueled by slave labor. In 1860 there were 4 million slaves in the United States — and 10 percent of them were in South Carolina. In fact, they made up 57 percent of the state's population. More than 400,000

African Americans in South Carolina were enslaved while a mere 10,000 of them were "free."

In Charleston, 36 percent of the city's 48,409 people were slaves, which represented a decline from past decades. The city was once the capital of the nation's slave trade, a place where 40 percent of the enslaved Africans in North America first landed in the New World. Charleston was built with slave labor and for nearly 200 years thrived on a slave economy.

South Carolina held such a concentration of slave labor because the Lowcountry's largest cash crop was rice, which required 10 times the labor needed to harvest, say, short staple cotton. By 1860 there were 14 men in the country who owned 500 or more slaves, and most of them lived in the Lowcountry. Slavery was almost wholly the domain of the very wealthy. Three percent of the white population owned 95 percent of the enslaved people in the country. This 3 percent, however, held a considerable majority of the state's political platform – and immeasurable sway with its citizens.

In 1835, when northern abolitionists began mailing "the proceedings of the Anti-Slavery Society of New York" to Charleston residents, politicians stirred the locals into a rage. One night a mob of several hundred people broke into the Exchange Building to stop the spread of this propaganda. They stole all the mail in the building and burned it on The Citadel's parade ground, not bothering to sort out the anti-slavery literature. Postmaster Alfred Huger was so incensed that he began to stand guard over the mail with a shotgun in hand.

Despite – or perhaps because of – its attitudes toward slavery and its role in the slave trade, Charleston was one of the more diverse cities in the South. The city's elite, largely made up of plantation owners who lived in Charleston part time, mingled in exclusive clubs and societies. But downtown was also the home of working-class whites — bakers, cobblers, blacksmiths, artisans. Just below them on the social ladder were free African Americans. A large portion of the state's free black population lived in Charleston, some of them the illegitimate children of slaves and their masters. And then there were the slaves themselves.

Some of these enslaved African Americans worked as servants in the city's mansions, but just as many could be seen on any given day in the city market, selling their own wares or produce from their owners' farms. Many even worked as artisans or laborers, although their pay went to their owners. There were restrictions on where these slaves could be in the city at any particular time, and they had to carry papers or tags so that they were easily identified (free blacks also had to carry papers to avoid confusion or arrest).

The men who owned these slaves were among South Carolina's most powerful politicians. No other state had such a large contingent of slave owners in its Legislature. From the point of view of many politicians in Washington, however, the city's — and much of the South's — ways had passed. This was never more evident than in April 1860, when Charleston had hosted the Democratic National Convention at Institute Hall.

Mercury owner Robert Barnwell Rhett

It was a disaster of sectional rivalry.

Massachusetts politician Caleb Cushing, a former U.S. attorney general and congressman, was elected presiding officer of the convention, and from his opening remarks took aim at the convention's hosts.

"Ours, gentlemen, is the motto inscribed on that scroll in the hands of the monumental statue of the great statesman of South Carolina — 'Truth, Justice and the Constitution,'" Cushing said. "Opposed to us are those who labor to overthrow the Constitution, under the false and insidious pretense of supporting it; those who are aiming to produce in this country a permanent sectional conspiracy of one-half of the states of the union against the other half — those who, impelled by a stupid and half insane spirit of faction and fanaticism, would hurry our land on to revolution and civil war."

The convention was doomed from the start. The Southerners demanded a party platform that would protect slavery; Northerners refused. Delegates from seven Southern states walked out, convening their own meeting at St. Andrew's Hall. The remaining delegates continued without them, arguing over a nominee for a week. The Northerners wanted Stephen Douglas, who had defeated Lincoln for his Senate seat two years earlier; the remaining Southerners wanted Breckinridge, at that time the vice president. Neither side would relent. The delegates finally gave up.

The Northern Democrats later reconvened in Baltimore and nominated Douglas. The Southerners, including Rhett, held a separate convention in Richmond that summer, where they nominated Breckinridge. In effect they split the national ticket, practically ensuring Lincoln's election. Two years earlier, in the speech that alerted Southerners to Lincoln's politics, the candidate — paraphrasing the New Testament — had said that "a house divided against itself cannot stand."

The Democrats themselves were fulfilling that prophecy: dividing themselves and dividing the country.

The rhetoric of secession grew more violent as the summer of 1860 wore on, no doubt spurred in part by the *Mercury's* constant editorializing. By October military leaders were recommending that President Buchanan install garrisons in all Southern forts because the threats to the federal government had become so harsh. No one knew this better than Abner Doubleday, a U.S. Army captain stationed at Fort Moultrie.

Doubleday had never made a secret of his anti-slavery sentiments, but the people of Charleston had recently become incensed by "offensive articles" on the subject of abolition that appeared in northern newspapers under his byline. Doubleday was perplexed – he had not written the articles, but his protests mattered little to locals. He was, without a doubt, one of these "Black Republicans."

Years later Doubleday would claim that the New York *Tribune* had an abolitionist reporter in Charleston posing as a secessionist – and working for Rhett's *Mercury*. The reporter, Doubleday claimed, later confessed to writing the abolitionist articles. It was an unsurprising revelation. There seemed no end to the covert machinations at work in the city as the fall of 1860 arrived.

The presidential election led to an immediate escalation of this tension. In the days following Lincoln's victory, the *Mercury* beat the drums of secession through Charleston. On Thursday, Nov. 8, the paper's lead headline declared that, as a result of the election, "The States Rights Flag Thrown to the Breeze." This warning was the talk of Charleston. In conversations around town, locals swore they would resist Lincoln's rule "at all hazards." The *Mercury* gleefully reported many such overheard conversations and idle threats. No doubt, Rhett's seeds of discontent had taken root.

The newspaper reported that most people thought "the South would soon govern the South."

"The tea of 1860 has been thrown overboard — the revolution of 1860 has been initiated," the *Mercury* gloated.

For the rest of the week, Charleston was overwhelmed by impromptu meetings, strategy sessions and even a rally outside City Hall. The wife of one United States senator, who arrived in town the day after the election, later wrote that she could hear the men's excited conversations one floor below her hotel room.

"The noise of the speaking and cheering was pretty hard on a tired traveler," Mary Boykin Chesnut wrote. "Suddenly, I found myself listening with pleasure. Voice, tone, temper, sentiment, language — all were perfect."

On Nov. 10 the state Legislature called for a convention on Dec. 17 "to take into consideration ... their relations with the Federal Government." At a ceremony to ratify the convention a few days later, a triumphant Barnwell Rhett set the tone for the meeting. He was almost giddy with excitement. After decades of efforts, he had the attention of his state – and the entire South.

In his speech that day, Rhett outlined the numerous sins the North had perpetuated against the South: It had invited foreigners to settle the territories bought in the Louisiana Purchase to dilute the power of the Southern states in Congress. It had initially declined to admit Missouri to the Union because it "tolerated slavery." It had imposed tariffs on the South that exclusively benefited Northern interests. For all those reasons, Rhett declared, the South should withdraw from the Union much as the United States had withdrawn from Britain.

The South could form its own nation, Rhett said, and three principles should guide the new country: slavery should be permitted, powers of taxation should be limited and "the forts and fortresses in our bay should never again be surrendered to any power on earth."

"My friends, the Union is dissolved," Rhett said. "The long weary night of our humiliation, oppression and danger is passing away, and the glorious dawn of a Southern Confederacy breaks on our view. With the blessing of God, we will soon be a great people — happy, prosperous and free."

All that remained was for one state to take the first step.

CHARLESTON

MERCURY

EXTRA:

Passed unanimously at 1.15 o'clock, P. M. December 20th, 1860.

AN ORDINANCE

To dissolve the Union between the State of South Carolina and other States united with her under the compact entitled " The Constitution of the United States of America."

We, the People of the State of South Carolina, in Convention assembled, do declare and ordain, and it is hereby declared and ordained,

That the Ordinance adopted by us in Convention, on the twenty-third day of May, in the year of our Lord one thousand seven hundred and eighty-eight, whereby the Constitution of the United States of America was ratified, and also, all Acts and parts of Acts of the General Assembly of this State, ratifying amendments of the said Constitution, are hereby repealed; and that the union now subsisting between South Carolina and other States, under the name of " The United States of America," is hereby dissolved.

THE

UNION

IS

DISSOLVED!

CHAPTER 2

'THE UNION IS DISSOLVED'

I t had all come down to this moment.

Robert Barnwell Rhett sat in the grand meeting room at St. Andrew's Hall occasionally gazing through an arched window as he waited for his name to be called. It was just after 1 p.m. on Dec. 20, 1860, and — decades after he had first championed the idea — South Carolina was seceding from the United States of America.

So much had happened in a few short weeks. Since the election of Abraham Lincoln, Charleston had been abuzz with the coming "Convention of the People of South Carolina," as the *Mercury* called it. There had been meetings nearly every night, locals plotting their next moves, speculating on how Washington would react to their secession — which most people now accepted as a foregone conclusion. The state would not remain in the Union with Lincoln as its president. The actual vote seemed little more than a formality.

The convention had opened in Columbia three days earlier, but panic over an alleged outbreak of smallpox sent the delegates scrambling for the train to Charleston. Some suspected that the smallpox scare was just an excuse to move the delegates to a much friendlier environment for secession. Either way, Rhett likely found it fitting that the ordinance he had promoted for years would be approved on Broad Street, barely a half-dozen blocks from the offices of the *Mercury*, the newspaper he owned.

Rhett listened carefully as John Inglis called the names of convention delegates: "Bonneau ... Brabham ... Brown ..."

Every call was answered with "Aye."

Inglis, a Maryland native now living in Chesterfield County, had been appointed chairman of the committee that drafted the ordinance. It was not a difficult task, in part because the panel used a document that Rhett – in a fit of optimism – had prepared long before the convention. It sped the process along considerably.

"Middleton ... Miles," Inglis continued. "Palmer ... Porcher."

Over the years Rhett had fallen in and out of favor for his views — some thought him a visionary, others believed him a hopeless extremist. But all that had changed since the election. For a while there had even been rumors that he would be elected governor of South Carolina, but that talk had been quickly silenced. He did not campaign for the job, perhaps because he had designs on another office.

Finally, Inglis called Rhett's name. In the silence of St. Andrew's Hall, he savored the moment before answering.

"Aye."

South Carolina's secession convention had dragged on for days.

At first the delegates had been bogged down with bureaucratic parliamentary procedure and a handful of trivial matters — what to do with federal employees working in the state, how to handle mail service. They even debated whether to allow reporters into the chamber. Rhett, himself a delegate, had no reason to be overly concerned with the *Mercury's* access. Although some members protested, most delegates argued that barring newspapers from the room would look bad. It would appear they were ashamed of what they were doing – and they certainly were not ashamed.

They fully believed they were doing the will of the people.

For proof, they only had to look beyond South Carolina's border. In the weeks since the election, several other Southern states — Mississippi, Alabama, Florida and Georgia among them — had begun planning their own conventions. Representatives of at least two of those states were in the audience to assure the men that if South Carolina seceded, it would not stand alone for long. Some of the state's delegates would be appointed to coordinate with these states, sort of like ambassadors. Already, there was talk of forming a confederacy.

At the same time, Rhett was selected to join a delegation that would travel to Washington and negotiate a settlement of all debts between the state and the U.S. government. Among other issues, these delegates would deliver terms for the government to turn over all federal property in the state – particularly the forts surrounding

Charleston Harbor. The United States would no longer be welcome to hold property in South Carolina, especially military installations.

Of course, first there was the actual business of seceding. The ordinance itself, which the delegation would carry to Washington, was so simple that the men gathered in St. Andrew's Hall had little need to debate it. It was elegantly short, designed to eventually fit on a single sheet of parchment. The document read:

"AN ORDINANCE to dissolve the union between the State of South Carolina and other States united with her under the compact entitled 'The Constitution of the United States of America.'

"We, the people of the State of South Carolina, in convention assembled, do declare and ordain, and it is hereby declared and ordained, That the ordinance adopted by us in convention on the twenty-third day of May, in the year of our Lord one thousand seven hundred and eighty-eight, whereby the Constitution of the United States of America was ratified, and also all acts and parts of acts of the General Assembly of this State ratifying amendments of the said Constitution, are hereby repealed; and that the union now subsisting between South Carolina and other States, under the name of the 'United States of America,' is hereby dissolved.

"Done at Charleston the twentieth day of December, in the year of our Lord one thousand eight hundred and sixty."

It took less than 10 minutes to call the roll. When Inglis finished at 1:15 p.m., the vote was 169-0.

Within minutes of the vote, the *Mercury* had a special edition circulating on the streets of Charleston. Its banner headline — destined to become an iconic symbol of the coming conflict — was even simpler than the ordinance. When the residents of Charleston read the news, the paper later reported, "loud shouts of joy rent the air." The headline declared:

"The UNION is DISSOLVED!"

As word of the vote spread through Charleston, church bells rang and businesses suspended trade. The Citadel fired artillery salutes, volunteers donned the uniforms of local militia and new flags were unfurled. The officers of the Lower Guard House stretched a line from their station to City Hall and used it to hang a banner that featured a palmetto with a rattlesnake coiled around it, cannons on either side. The names of 15 Southern states surrounded the palmetto, along with the words "Hope," "Faith" and "Southern Republic."

The *Mercury* reported "(a)t the base of the arch the non-slaveholding states are represented divided and broken into fragments, and underneath the whole of the motto, 'Built from the ruins,' indicative of the position of South Carolina and the Southern Confederacy."

According to the newspaper, the entire community was overjoyed by the vote. But in some corners of the city a few people were less than enthusiastic. One man saved his special edition of the *Mercury*, which would eventually find its way into the collection of the Charleston Museum. At the bottom of the paper, the man wrote, "You'll regret the day you ever done it. I preserve this to see how it ends."

James Louis Petigru was certainly not happy, either. The veteran politician – dean of the South Carolina Bar, the man who had successfully defeated Rhett and the "test oath" in court decades earlier – feared for his state. Days earlier when the Secession Convention had been meeting in Columbia, Petigru – who was there on business – had been stopped by a stranger and asked for directions to the city's insane asylum. He told the man that the building was on the outskirts of town and then pointed to First Baptist Church, where the convention was meeting, adding "but I think you will find the inmates yonder."

He would hone that quip into one of the greatest quotes in South Carolina political history within a week. But very few shared Petigru's sense of foreboding; most, in fact, were ecstatic. Mary Boykin Chesnut would soon mock him publicly, noting that "Mr. Petigru has such a keen sense of the ridiculous he must be laughing in his sleeve at the hubbub this untimely trait of independence has raised."

To be sure, Petigru held the minority view in Charleston. Most locals saw secession as a step into the light of freedom and independence, words that evoked strong emotional responses. South Carolinians had been told by their politicians that a minority was controlling the majority, and that wasn't the way the United States had been designed to work. Such was the rhetoric that secessionists used to rally the masses, but there were more specific reasons.

Those were evident in the "Declarations of Causes Which Justify the Secession of

Institute Hall, renamed Secession Hall, was next to the Circular Congregational Church on Meeting Street and was the setting for the signing of the Ordinance of Secession.

South Carolina from the Federal Union," a report written by a committee of delegates in the days after the vote – with significant influence by Rhett. The document recounted the entire history of the United States from the adoption of the Constitution forward, with much attention to the rights of sovereignty and self-government given to the states. Reading the report, C.G. Memminger spoke of "an increasing hostility on the part of the Northern States to the institution of slavery" that had led to their disregard of sovereignty. He spoke of federal laws that once supported slavery now being used against the institution.

"These states have assumed the right of deciding upon the propriety of our domestic institutions; and have denied the rights of property established in fifteen of the States and recognized by the Constitution; they have denounced as sinful the institution of slavery."

The report was so heavily laced with slavery rhetoric – with nearly 20 references to the "peculiar institution" – that another delegate, Maxcy Gregg, stood up and

Engraving from the December 1, 1860 edition of *Frank Leslie's Illustrated Newspaper* depicting a secession rally in front of the Mills House in Charleston.

complained that "not one word is said about the tariff, which for so many years caused a contest in this State against the Federal Government."

Gregg referred to the 1828 "Tariff of Abominations," which had been the origin of the state's first threat to secede during the nullification crisis. Three decades later, some South Carolinians still harbored a grudge – and no doubt some delegates believed it to be a more pertinent, and over-arching, issue than slavery. Several delegates wanted a new report that would blame tariffs as the predominant reason for secession. They introduced a motion to table Memminger's report – the first sign of division in the convention.

The delegates had agreed to cast a unanimous vote for the secession itself, but they could not fully agree on their reason. While Rhett and Memminger were content to blame the secession on threats to slavery, Gregg had at least two dozen delegates on his side, men who considered tariffs their greatest concern. Their attempts to reframe the secession and the coming conflict failed. The convention had been stacked with wealthy landowners – and slaveholders – which made the outcome a foregone conclusion. The motion to table Memminger's report was defeated by a 4-to-1 margin. The convention's secretary would not record which members voted to amend the report.

Williams Middleton, owner of Middleton Place, was certainly among the delegates who favored naming U.S. slavery policy as the cause of secession. Williams and his brother John Izard Middleton, who owned a plantation in Georgetown and was also a delegate, held hundreds of enslaved African Americans. These slaves cultivated Middleton rice using practices carried over from Africa, and had become self-sufficient at harvesting all of the plantations' crops. They also managed the plantations' considerable collections of livestock, often supervising themselves. The Middletons' entire livelihood depended upon this slave labor, and it was the perceived threats to the institution that had convinced them that South Carolina must secede.

Other delegates worried about how inflammatory the Memminger report might appear to outsiders. They wanted to soften it, to downplay the role of slavery in their decision, if for no other reason than to make it more palatable to nations they would soon court for diplomatic relations. But men such as the Middletons held the most sway at the convention, and Memminger's report was adopted.

The report was accepted by a voice vote on Christmas Eve — a move, historians would note, that left it unclear how many delegates actually voted to name slavery as the main cause of secession. But it was a majority. According to Rhett biographer William C. Davis, Rhett did not consider slavery "the root cause of secession in his mind," but he felt it "was certainly the occasion that brought it about."

In fact, Rhett found Memminger's version of the report tame.

More than 3,000 people lined the streets of downtown Charleston that evening, eager to catch a glimpse of history. At 6:30 the delegates finally appeared outside St. Andrew's Hall, prompting a loud cheer from the raucous crowd. There had been considerable debate over when and where to sign the actual ordinance. A few delegates wanted to delay the signing until the next day at noon, which would allow time to have the ordinance printed on parchment. But a majority did not want to wait — it had been passed on Dec. 20 and they wanted to sign it on Dec. 20. Enthusiasm and impatience won out.

The ordinance was rushed to a printer that afternoon, and he was persuaded to have it ready that evening. Later, each member would receive his own copy – but only after the signing ceremony. The delegates fell in a loose line and solemnly marched east on Broad Street. When they reached the intersection of Meeting Street, the men turned north. The *Mercury* later would describe the sight of this parade as "grand and impressive."

"There were a people assembled through their highest representatives — men most of them upon whose heads the snows of sixty winters had been shed — the dignitaries of the land — the High Priests of the Church of Christ — revered statesmen — and the wise judges of the law," the paper proclaimed.

The parade ended at Institute Hall, an Italianate building just six years old that stood next to the Circular Congregational Church. In its short history the complex had been the site of fairs and concerts; the building's Grand Hall seated 3,000 people. That was not nearly enough space for all the people who wanted to witness the signing, but it was Charleston's largest public venue and would have to suffice. In a burst of patriotism, the building was renamed "Secession Hall."

Inside, the ceremony began with the Rev. John Bachman offering a prayer about "this great act ... about to be consummated." Then the convention's president, David F. Jamison of Barnwell, read the ordinance off the parchment.

By the time Jamison reached the word "dissolved," the *Mercury* said, the crowd erupted — the "men could contain themselves no longer, and a shout that shook the very building, reverberating, long-continued, rose to Heaven, and ceased only with the loss of breath."

The delegates lined up in the alphabetical order of the districts they represented to wait their turn with the document. The actual signing took two hours. As each man wrote his name on the parchment, the cheers increased throughout the hall. By the time Rhett reached the Ordinance, the *Mercury* later reported, the shouts had become deafening.

When Rhett stepped up to the table, he dropped to his knees and bowed his head – a bit of showmanship for the crowd. But for him it truly was a dramatic moment; he had waited nearly his entire life for this. He signed his name under Memminger's, "R. Barnwell Rhett," and soon after that, it was done.

South Carolina had officially, irrevocably, seceded from the Union.

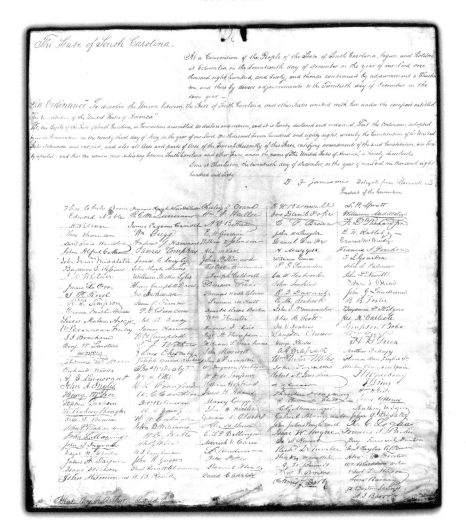

South Carolina's Ordinance of Secession
South Carolina Department of History and Archives image

Major Robert Anderson, U.S.A.

CHAPTER 3

ACTS OF WAR

A gray fog rolled through Charleston on Christmas Day – a heavy blanket that smothered the city and left evergreens "coated with uncomfortable moisture." Cold rain blew in off the harbor and only muddy children who managed to "escape the parental roof" and sneak outside to roam damp sidewalks stirred in the streets, where they gazed at festive decorations in misty shop windows.

The *Mercury* reported that "the elements had conspired to make the merriest day of all the year the most gloomy and forbidding."

The city was quiet in the week following the secession vote. After the pomp and circumstance of the ordinance signing, little changed noticeably in the city. The newspaper reported that each day more federal employees resigned their commission, choosing state over nation. But other than the occasional unveiling of a new flag or banner, most of Charleston's attention turned to the holidays. As the ramifications of the state's secession spread across the country, South Carolina awaited news from the delegation to Washington. Robert Barnwell Rhett and a group of men were in the capital trying to negotiate a peaceful transfer of federal property within the state's borders. Slowly, South Carolina was cutting all ties to the Union.

The secession was a leap of faith, but the news in the *Mercury* reinforced local opinion that South Carolina would not stand alone for long. Every day reports filtered into the city that other states were planning their own secession conventions — six in January alone. Florida would meet just after the New Year, while Mississippi and Alabama would decide concurrently on Jan. 7. Texas, Georgia and Louisiana would follow by the month's end. North Carolina was still pondering its next move.

All of this suggested that 1861 would be an eventful year, but it appeared the remainder of 1860 would pass quietly. South Carolina merely had to endure a few weeks in a political limbo, its future as murky as its streets. The *Mercury* noted that neither this fact nor the weather did much to quell the holiday spirit for most of the city's residents.

"Within doors there was the usual frolic and enjoyment, and the fact that they were no longer people of the United States did not diminish a whit of the zest with which people relished their turkeys and demolished their plum puddings and mince pies," the paper reported. "We venture to predict that next Christmas they will eat them with a still keener enjoyment."

It would be the last peaceful Christmas in Charleston for five years. Within two days, the entire city would be consumed by rumors of a coming war.

Maj. Robert Anderson was worried.

The new commander at Fort Moultrie had been on the job little more than a month and in that time everything had changed. He had monitored the events in Charleston closely and was disturbed by the state's open animosity toward the United States and its military. His orders from Washington were vague, and he increasingly felt alone and vulnerable. Still, for a while he had kept the fort's gates open to anyone who wanted to wander in – a symbolic gesture perhaps.

By mid-December, nefarious rumors forced Anderson to reconsider that decision. First, he heard that the state's militia had moved cannons to the north end of Sullivan's Island to fire on any ship that might attempt to deliver provisions to Moultrie. Then his troops received word that 2,000 of the state's finest riflemen had been dispatched to the houses and dunes surrounding the fort, their guns trained on the parapet, ready to shoot at the first sign of action.

Even if Anderson was inclined to dismiss such stories as fanciful conspiracies, he could not ignore the *Mercury*. The newspaper had begun to publish detailed diagrams of the harbor forts on its front pages — this in a newspaper that seldom, if ever, used illustrations. What purpose could that serve? Nothing good, Anderson concluded.

Anderson, 56, was a most unlikely candidate to be in such a position. A thoughtful, intelligent man, the Kentucky native was a Southerner to the core and may have even felt a kinship with the South Carolinians lurking around his fort. After all, they held a shared history. His father had defended Moultrie during the Revolutionary War and was a prisoner of war during the British occupation of the city.

In his long military career, Anderson had fought the Seminoles in Florida more than 20 years earlier and served with Abraham Lincoln in the Black Hawk Indian war of 1832 – and was honored for his actions in both conflicts. He was, in short, a hero. Even the *Mercury* fawned over Anderson when it reported on actions at the fort. The difference between Anderson and his Charleston admirers was the major's abiding loyalty to the United States. Although he was decidedly pro-slavery, as most wealthy Southerners were, Anderson thought this secession business was dangerous – the work of extremists. And he worried about what acts of extremism these South Carolinians might inspire next.

Soon after the secession vote James Louis Petigru, the city's most famous dissenter, visited the Moultrie troops. The man who days earlier had proclaimed that "South Carolina is too small for a republic and too large for a lunatic asylum" greeted the soldiers with a tear in his eye. He reported that the rumors were true – plans were indeed underway to drive them from the fort. Capt. Abner Doubleday would later recall that Petigru made it clear he "deplored the folly and the madness of the times." But the old judge knew he could not stop it. Petigru simply wanted to bid them farewell, as if the outcome were all but certain.

The news came as no surprise to Anderson. It was reasonable to assume Moultrie might be a target – the fort was a symbol of the state and its independence dating back to the days when his father had served there. It was hallowed ground for locals, the place from which their ancestors had famously repelled the British in the early days of the American Revolution. The latest incarnation of the fort was more than 50 years old but still a potent force. Situated on the southern end of Sullivan's, it was in perfect position to defend the channel leading into Charleston Harbor. But it was never intended to defend itself from the very people it was supposed to protect.

The walls at Moultrie were notoriously low, and dunes had built up against some walls to the point that an occasional cow wandered onto the parapet. Even worse, Moultrie was woefully undermanned. Designed to house 300 men, there were fewer than 100 U.S. soldiers stationed at the fort in December 1860. As the rumors of hostilities persisted, those men tried their best to reinforce Moultrie, filling crevices in the wall and digging a ditch around it that made those walls 16 feet high. A makeshift

Maj. Anderson's federal troops retreat from Fort Moultrie to Fort Sumter.

picket fence was hung over the side of the parapet as a further barricade to anyone attempting to scale the walls.

Although Anderson's men had modified Moultrie admirably, they realized the more defensible position lay just across the channel. But when the troops suggested abandoning Moultrie for Fort Sumter, Anderson calmly said his orders were to defend Fort Moultrie – even though he privately felt the same way.

Fort Sumter was an intimidating presence. It was built on a manmade island and designed to house 650 soldiers and more than 130 guns. The fort's five walls towered 50 feet over the water as if they had sprung from the sea – which, in a sense, they had. Sumter was solid and menacing, and Charleston Harbor acted as its formidable, and natural, moat. The only trouble was that it had not yet been finished.

Named for Revolutionary War hero Thomas Sumter, the Carolina Gamecock, construction had begun in 1829. But more than 30 years later, the fort sat unoccupied with a partial complement of guns and brick layers. Construction workers were the only personnel. Following the secession vote, that is exactly how South Carolina

expected it to remain – unfinished. State officials claimed they had assurances from the federal government that no troops would occupy Sumter. Anderson would later say he knew nothing of any such agreement.

Late on the afternoon of Dec. 26, 1860, Anderson had finally had enough. If Moultrie was attacked, he knew it would be a slaughter. So despite the diplomatic implications, Anderson made the decision — on his own, he later maintained — to move his base of operations to Sumter. Anderson found what he considered a loop-hole in his orders. Although he had been assigned to Moultrie, he was ostensibly in charge of all fortifications in Charleston. He reasoned that, with such latitude, he could occupy whichever fort he pleased.

Until the last possible moment, Anderson kept the decision largely to himself, telling only a few officers charged with getting the women and children out of the fort. He did this to ensure word of his plan would not leak. No one at Moultrie would have willingly betrayed the plans, but sometimes word just had a way of leaking out. Doubleday suspected something was afoot.

The day before the evacuation, Doubleday asked if he might buy some wire to make an entanglement in front of his battery – just another barrier to slow down any attackers. Major Anderson told him to buy a mile of wire if he so desired. But when the captain said he'd send for it immediately, Anderson "objected in such a peculiar way that I at once saw that he was no longer interested in our efforts to strengthen Fort Moultrie."

After dinner on the 26th, Doubleday made his way onto the fort's parapet to invite Anderson to take tea with his men. There he found the major surrounded by a group of officers. The men acted odd, and said little when Doubleday greeted them. It was an awkward moment until Anderson declared, "I have determined to evacuate this post immediately." Doubleday had 20 minutes to get his men ready.

Most of Anderson's troops snuck out at nightfall, making their way to boats hidden behind a pile of rocks on the back side of the island. Five men stayed on the shore to cover the boats in case Southern troops tried to stop them, their guns aimed at the channel leading to Sumter. It was a prudent precaution, but proved unnecessary. No one would witness Anderson's retreat from Fort Moultrie.

It was not an entirely easy crossing. On the short trip to Sumter, one of the boats carrying the federal troops spotted a Southern guard boat, but cut a wide path around it. The ever-cautious Doubleday had his men take off their coats and use them to cover their muskets. He hoped that they might pass for laborers returning to the fort.

"It was after sunset, and the twilight had deepened, so that there was a fair chance for us to escape," Doubleday later said. "While the steamer was yet far off, I took off my cap, and threw open my coat to conceal the buttons."

The men on the guard boat never saw them.

The troops who remained at Moultrie spiked the cannons, driving plugs into the guns' touch holes to prevent them from being fired, and then burned the wooden carriages that held them. Finally, Anderson's troops sawed down Moultrie's flag staff and made their escape. They had left the fort a wreck.

It was the next morning before anyone noticed anything was amiss.

On Dec. 27, the city awoke to panic.

Rumors of the previous night's events spread quickly, but the stories were so muddled and contradictory that the *Mercury* reported "it was no easy matter to get at the

Spiking the cannon at Fort Moultrie.

truth." Locals made their way to The Battery to see what was happening on Sullivan's Island, some racing to the tops of buildings, a few even climbing the bell rooms of the Holy City's church steeples. A couple of men brought their own telescopes. At first there was little to see — smoke pouring from Moultrie's ramparts covered the horizon. Through the haze, however, someone spotted a small group of men at Fort Sumter unloading supplies from a schooner. Slowly the picture came into focus.

"The ladies, who had hitherto lived in the fort (Moultrie), had been previously sent to Charleston, and, whatever furniture, ammunition and provisions that could be moved without exciting suspicion, had been quietly transferred to Fort Sumter," the *Mercury* reported on Dec. 28. "The report that the defences of Fort Moultrie had been so shamefully mutilated naturally aroused great indignation in the city."

A reporter from the *Mercury* reached Moultrie early on the afternoon of Dec. 27. By then state troops had taken control of the fort and refused to allow him inside. From what he could see, however, it looked as if Moultrie had been ransacked. The

Evacuation of Fort Moultrie, and burning of the gun carriages, on Sullivan's Island.

island seemed oddly quiet, the reporter later noted. Perhaps that was because South Carolina's retaliation would come from elsewhere.

That afternoon, Col. J.J. Pettigrew of the 1st South Carolina Rifles gathered 150 men at The Citadel. He told these troops — some from the Washington Light Infantry, others from the Meagher Guards or the Carolina Infantry — only that he had a mission for them and that he was acting on orders of Gov. Francis Pickens. Pettigrew then marched the men to a wharf on the Cooper River where they boarded the steamer *Nina* – one of the guard boats that Anderson's men had slipped past the night before. Shortly after the *Nina* cast off, it became clear to most of the troops that they were headed directly for Castle Pinckney.

The small fort on Shutes' Folly Island, named for the local Revolutionary hero Charles Cotesworth Pinckney, stood barely a mile from the Charleston peninsula. The fort, which dated to 1810, was built atop the remains of an older outpost that was designed to protect the city when war with the French appeared imminent. On that day, Pinckney was occupied only by U.S. Army Lt. R.K. Meade and a couple dozen laborers — not exactly a fighting force. Anderson sent Meade to Pinckney but the lieutenant could not persuade the workers to learn basic weaponry, which left the fort practically defenseless.

As the *Nina* approached the Shutes' Folly dock, the troops could see a man on shore waiting to greet them. He was "observed holding what appeared to be a paper in his hand," the *Mercury* later reported. "This was said to be the Riot Act."

The gate to Pinckney was locked but that did little to stop the Southerners. Pettigrew sent a few men to fetch storming ladders from the *Nina* and, when they returned, he ordered them to scale the fort's walls. Soon the gate was opened and 150 South Carolina soldiers rushed inside to find the surprised laborers. Pettigrew approached Meade and immediately began to read Gov. Pickens' order, but the lieutenant stopped him.

He would not recognize the governor's authority to take control of the fort, Meade said, but neither would he fight it. Pettigrew allowed the man to gather his personal belongings and watched as Meade set out in a small boat for Sumter. A reporter on the scene said a red flag sporting a white star was taken off the *Nina* and hoisted over Pinckney. By the time the journalist left "a strong guard had been mounted, and preparations for garrisoning the fort were well advanced."

It was a rather peaceful coup, but historians later would cite the taking of Castle Pinckney as the first overt act of war between South Carolina and the federal government. Southerners, however, considered Anderson's retreat to Sumter the first act of aggression; they had only reacted to it. Like with so many things surrounding the events in Charleston that year, neither side would ever agree on much of anything.

Even after Sumter was occupied, the Charleston newspapers refused to speak ill of Anderson or question his decision from a military point of view — perhaps it was Southern courtesy. But they claimed the symbolism of his actions spoke volumes about the state's predicament and proved the secessionists' claims that the United States harbored hostile attitudes toward the South.

"The events of the past few weeks, and the developments they have occasioned, have served, in a remarkable degree, to clear up and remove all doubts concerning the designs and temper of the North towards the South," the *Mercury* opined.

In the final days of 1860, the *Mercury* reiterated the secessionists' arguments against the United States: the North meant to force higher taxes upon the South and

Fort Sumter in Charleston Harbor

end slavery. Robert Barnwell Rhett Jr. argued in an editorial that if the North was so opposed to the peculiar institution, secession should have relieved its consciences of the "dreadful moral responsibility – simply by quitting the connection."

Instead, it appeared that the North was determined to hold its ground and impose its will, and its whims, on the South.

"The question not only of self-respect, but of self-preservation, is forced upon the people of the Southern states," Rhett wrote.

After South Carolina claimed Castle Pinckney, volunteer troops set up outside the U.S. Arsenal overlooking the river at Ashley Avenue near the intersection of Mill Street. They were ordered to stop any shipment of ammunition or weapons to Fort Sumter. The Palmetto Guard and cadet riflemen worked a shift, and then were relieved by the Irish Volunteers. In turn, the German Fusiliers took over for the Irish. No one entered or exited the building for the next several days. There were rumors that some of the ammunition had been destroyed by the federal troops barricaded inside, but the *Mercury* reported that those stories were "wholly without foundation."

The standoff would last only a few days. On Dec. 30, Col. John Cunningham of the 17th Infantry Regiment delivered a message from Gov. Pickens to arsenal personnel:

The governor demanded that the federal troops surrender the arsenal.

F.C. Humphreys, an ordnance sergeant temporarily in charge of the arsenal, admitted to Cunningham that he didn't have the manpower to fight, but he would comply only under protest. And only if he could salute the U.S. flag as it was lowered. Cunningham not only allowed the salute, he gave Humphreys permission to fire 32 guns as the flag went down, one for every state that remained in the Union – for the moment.

Following that ceremony, a Palmetto banner replaced the Stars and Stripes and as it flapped in the breeze, "a salute of cannon was fired to celebrate the event."

"We fancy that the guards will watch more zealously than ever, now that they know that the flag of their redeemed country is floating proudly over them," Rhett wrote in the *Mercury*.

As 1860 ended, South Carolina was a nation unto itself. In addition to Moultrie, Pinckney and the arsenal, state troops had taken control of the U.S. Post Office and the entire Exchange Building. Even the *Daily Courier*, Charleston's more even-handed newspaper, could not ignore the implications.

On the final day of 1860, the *Courier* reported, "The people of South Carolina have thus taken the first step in civil war."

The Star of the West approaches Charleston Harbor.

CHAPTER 4

THE BEST LAID PLANS

The ship cut through the water slowly, the haze and black Atlantic night conspiring to make it nearly impossible to see.

It arrived outside Charleston Harbor around 1:30 a.m., the captain surprised to discover that all the city's navigational lights had been extinguished. He searched for the channel with only a thin sliver of moon for light, to no avail. They were sailing blind in unfamiliar water, their destination only a few miles away. For several hours the ship crept forward with a crew on deck to take constant soundings. Most times they measured the same depth: four-and-a-half fathoms, or about 27 feet. They were, it appeared, on the right course.

The boat was a civilian steamship with two masts and a side paddle wheel. It left New York on Jan. 5, and to any casual observer it appeared to be just another commercial steamship — one more merchant vessel surfing the Gulf Stream. Later the captain would report that the voyage South had been pleasant, given the season. All of that changed when they reached Charleston and the absence of channel lights cost them any chance for a clandestine night landing.

As the first strains of daylight broke over the Atlantic, the ship had made enough progress that it was nearly within a half-mile of Morris Island and in sight of its ultimate destination. There was a steamer just ahead, nearly two miles off the bow. It signaled the shore with blue and red lights before crossing the bar and sailing into the channel – a local boat, the captain assumed. He decided to follow its course, but not before ordering all his passengers – dozens of federal soldiers – to get out of sight below deck. He gave the order to proceed and the ship lurched toward the channel, only a couple of miles from Fort Sumter.

And then someone opened fire.

The first shot sailed over the top of the ship. Another buzzed the pilot house, and a third barely missed the smokestack. The next shot found its mark, hitting the ship aft of the foremast and crashing through the deck. Moments later, a fifth missed the ship's rudder "by an ace," the captain would later claim.

The crew scrambled immediately, some startled by the hit, others running to assess the damage. In the confusion Capt. John McGowan glanced over at Morris Island, obviously the origin of the attack. He spotted a large banner flying above the dunes – a dark red flag with a white palmetto on it. It was Jan. 9, 1861, and the *Star of the West* had just sailed into a war zone.

The sentries on Morris Island had spotted the ship just after reveille. They were not surprised — they had, in fact, been expecting it. Rumors of the *Star of the West's* mission had been circulating through Charleston for days. Northern newspapers had reported that the federal government hired the ship to deliver supplies, ammunition and several hundred troops to reinforce Sumter. But the men on Morris Island would not allow that to happen.

There were nearly 300 troops on the island that morning – most of them from local rifle regiments, as well as 40 cadets from The Citadel. They watched the *Star of the West* as it approached Morris Island on its way to dock at Sumter. They let the ship draw in closer, until it was well within range. Then, just after 7 a.m., Maj. P.F. Stephens ordered the cadets to fire a shot across the ship's bow, a warning that it should turn around. The cadet who pulled the lanyard was G.E. Haynsworth, and he would go down in local history as the man who fired the first shot of the American Civil War.

The troops watched for a reaction from the ship. They were patient, realizing it could take several minutes to turn a ship of its size. But the *Star of the West* never deviated from its course; it kept trudging forward. As Stephens watched for any sign of retreat he spotted an entirely unexpected reaction: The men on the ship's foremast hoisted a United States flag.

Stephens ordered his men to open fire.

McGowan had little working in his favor: he was outgunned, outflanked and running into shallow water. When the firing began, he ordered the crew to continue on course because he felt there was no other choice. If they stopped, the ship could drift and run aground in the outgoing tide. Getting stuck within firing range of Morris Island would have been a death sentence for the *Star of the West*.

The captain never considered fighting back. His ship was unarmed and, even if McGowan had guns, he knew that returning fire could start a war – and that was a responsibility he had not agreed to accept. Still, he would not give up easily. McGowan meant to reach Fort Sumter. But he soon realized that he had more problems than the Morris Island battery — and he was headed straight for them. In the distance McGowan spotted "a steamer approaching us with an armed schooner in tow." He assumed the ships meant to intercept him. While he was distracted by the warship off his bow, Fort Moultrie opened fire.

The *Mercury* would gush for more than a week about the "Heroism at Fort Moultrie" on that morning. The shots fired from Morris Island alerted the fort's troops that something was amiss and they quickly sprang into action. The men on Sullivan's Island had heard the rumors of a ship carrying provisions to Sumter and understood the consequences of allowing the *Star of the West* – which they knew could be carrying hundreds of federal troops – to reach Sumter.

The ship was an easy mark for the Sullivan's Island fort. To reach Fort Sumter, the *Star of the West* had to sail within a mile of Moultrie. But it was not that simple. If Sumter moved to defend the supply ship, the men at Fort Moultrie would face the full might of a superior fort that, even without a full complement of guns, could most likely kill them all. It was a dangerous predicament. But the state troops decided they must take the risk. If Sumter were resupplied, the odds against Fort Moultrie's survival dropped dramatically.

It was a short engagement. When Fort Moultrie opened fire, McGowan knew he had no choice but to retreat. He gave the order to turn back to sea and make its best possible speed to open water. Before the ship sailed beyond the range of the Sullivan's Island guns, two more shots hit the *Star of the West*.

Riding the outgoing tide, it took the ship about an hour to clear the bar, slip beyond the range of Moultrie's guns and reach open water. It would be nearly three hours before McGowan felt any relief, however, as a steamer from Charleston followed them

Maj. P.F. Stephens orders the Citadel cadets to fire a shot across the ship's bow.

over the horizon. The Southern ship broke off its pursuit when the *Star of the West* rendezvoused with its military escort ship, which was waiting far offshore. Once they reached the Gulf Stream, McGowan turned north and sailed for New York.

The incident caused a great stir in the North. The New York papers insisted that the firing on an unarmed ship was an overt act of war, and there was little disagreement in Southern journalism. Within a week, the *Mercury*'s ongoing accounts of the skirmish would carry the headline "The War Begun." McGowan and his crew did their best to downplay the incident, joking about it to reporters when they reached New York.

"The people of Charleston pride themselves upon their hospitality," one of the officers told the New York *Evening Post*, "but it exceeds my expectations. They gave us several balls before we landed."

The *Star of the West* had the misfortune of arriving in Charleston at a time when

locals were spoiling for a fight.

The day before the incident, the wives of the Fort Sumter officers had become so worried about local attitudes toward them that they left town. Abner Doubleday's wife tried to check into a downtown hotel, only to be told she must first obtain the "sanction" of Robert Barnwell Rhett Jr. – no one in the city wanted to raise the ire of the *Mercury* editor. Eventually, the boarding house keeper apologetically explained that she depended on Southern business and could not risk alienating potential customers by harboring the wives of federal soldiers.

The city had been on edge since the New Year in large part due to the news out of Washington. The *Mercury* reported that U.S. Secretary of War John B. Floyd had recommended the federal government abandon Sumter to "prevent civil war," which is exactly what South Carolina wanted. But President James Buchanan — Abraham Lincoln had been elected but not yet inaugurated — appeared disinclined to even consider such a notion.

Nor did the outgoing president show any interest in negotiating with Robert Barnwell Rhett, who had been sent to Washington to secure title to all U.S. property in the state, including lighthouses and forts. The *Mercury* kept the city informed of Rhett's progress, or the lack thereof, and suggested Buchanan's refusal to surrender Sumter constituted yet another "cause of war" – a sentiment echoed in editorials from the Richmond *Dispatch*, which the *Mercury* often reprinted. These southern papers were now predicting the federal government was taking steps to bring the country to war.

"What can be gained by attempting the recapture of Fort Moultrie, Castle Pinckney and the Charleston Arsenal?" the *Dispatch* asked. "Will their successful recapture bring back South Carolina into the Union, or prevent Florida, Alabama, Georgia, Mississippi, Louisiana, Texas, Arkansas, North Carolina, Tennessee and Virginia from going out?"

By Monday, Jan. 7, this growing tension finally led to bloodshed. Around 10 p.m., a sentinel at Castle Pinckney making his rounds was approached by an unidentified man. The soldier "presented his musket in the act of challenging him" when the gun accidentally fired. The anonymous man fell immediately.

The injured man was Pvt. R.L. Holmes of the Carolina Light Infantry, a native of the city not yet 30 years old. The ball had hit Holmes just below the left shoulder and ricocheted inside him, managing to puncture both his lungs. He died within 20 minutes. There officially was no war, but Charleston had suffered its first casualty. Before Holmes could be buried at Magnolia Cemetery, the troops on Morris Island would be firing on the *Star of the West*.

Little more than an hour after the *Star of the West* made its getaway, a small boat flying a white flag sailed from Sumter toward downtown Charleston. The man in the boat, a federal soldier named Hall, carried a letter from Maj. Robert Anderson that was addressed to the South Carolina governor. The Fort Sumter commander wanted clarification about the morning's events.

"Two of your batteries fired this morning upon an unarmed vessel bearing the flag of my Government," Anderson wrote. "As I have not been notified that war has been declared by South Carolina against the Government of the United States, I cannot think but that this hostile act was committed without your sanction or authority.

Under that hope, and that alone, did I refrain from opening fire upon your batteries."

His troops wanted to fire on the Morris Island guns but Anderson would not allow it. He desperately wanted to avoid the all-out war. But in truth, the incident happened so quickly there had been no time to react. Afterward, Anderson decided his only course of action was to send a letter to the governor.

Francis Pickens, no doubt discouraged by Rhett's lack of success in Washington, was condescending in his reply to Anderson. The note, which was reprinted in the *Mercury*, suggested that Anderson had not been "fully informed by your government of the precise relations between it and the State of South Carolina." Pickens said that Buchanan received a copy of the Ordinance of Secession and should understand that "sending any reinforcement of troops of the United States in the harbor of Charleston would be regarded by the constitutional authorities of the State of South Carolina, as an act of hostility."

The exchange would never be more than a footnote in history, but it foreshadowed a coming escalation of the situation in Charleston. Anderson suggested he would not hesitate to fire on South Carolina troops if provoked, and Pickens assured him that the state was no friend of the United States government.

On Jan. 21 a committee of legislators in Columbia presented a proposal for a national flag of South Carolina. Following the secession, officials had determined they must replace the United States flag with a banner that would identify the state and its new independent status. The committee report suggested "the National Flag or Ensign of South Carolina shall be white, with a green palmetto tree upright thereon; and the union blue, with a white increscent." No one was overly impressed by the idea.

Within a week, one senator would suggest they instead adopt a red flag that sported a green palmetto and brown trunk. The idea infuriated one House member: Robert Barnwell Rhett Jr. The *Mercury* editor used his newspaper to criticize the "calico appearance" of the proposed Senate flag, and made it clear he did not like the committee plan any better. He believed the South Carolina flag should be simple, elegant, even majestic. Rhett promoted his own idea for a flag – a two-color design that was at once beautiful and simple. The flag, he wrote, should be "blue with a white palmetto tree upright thereon, and a white crescent in the upper corner."

There would be dissenters, men who continued to promote their own designs, but none of those lawmakers had the public pulpit of Rhett, no way to fight a man who bought his ink by the barrel. On Jan. 28, the General Assembly fell in line with the newspaper editor, and South Carolina had its flag – one that it would continue to use for the next two centuries. But it would not serve as a "national" flag for long; soon it would become merely the state flag.

On Jan. 12 a *Mercury* headline reported "Alabama is out of the Union." Two days later, word reached Charleston that Florida had also seceded. In fact, Mississippi had been the second state to secede. The state voted to leave the Union on Jan. 9, just hours after the *Star of the West* incident. By the end of the month, Georgia, Louisiana and Texas followed suit, bringing the number of states that had seceded to seven.

It did not take long for the political leaders of those states to make plans to join forces. They agreed to meet Feb. 4 in Montgomery, Ala., with the "grave mission," as the *Mercury* reported, of "constructing a Confederate Government for those States which have seceded from the Union of the late United States."

Rhett, who was making no progress in Washington, traveled by train to the convention so that he could serve as one of South Carolina's delegates. From there, he would send dispatches to his son, who in turn would share the news with the people of Charleston through the *Mercury*. For a while, however, there was little to report. Delegates quickly dismissed any suggestion that they rejoin the Union and set about building what they considered a more perfect union. In those first weeks, there was rampant speculation about who would be chosen as the South's president. Rhett secretly coveted the spot, even thought he deserved it. After all, he had led the Southern states to this.

But Rhett was upset to learn that other members of the South Carolina delegation had already come to the conclusion that the new president should come from Georgia – perhaps to enhance enthusiasm for secession in that state. Not even Rhett's own colleagues appeared willing to support his candidacy, which soon gnawed at the fire-eater.

The Southerners wasted little time. Within a week the convention delegates had adopted a provisional constitution. Most of the document had been copied word-for-word from the U.S. Constitution – with provisions added to ensure states' rights and the legality of slavery. Perhaps in a nod to the tariff controversy of previous decades, the delegates decided their new government could not spend tax money from one state on projects in another. Southern states had long complained that the U.S. Congress spent a disproportionate amount of its revenues on Northern states. Some even cited it as a mitigating factor for secession.

Although the delegates repeatedly claimed their states had every legal right to secede, this new government would not be recognized diplomatically by the United States or any foreign nation, although many would trade with the South. This did little to abate the enthusiasm of the men in Montgomery, even though they disagreed on how the new government should work. They would remain in session for weeks to work out the details.

Rhett, realizing his dreams of the South's presidency were fading, attempted one final power play. He suggested sending commissioners to England and France before a new president could be elected. Rhett, of course, would control the committee – and shape policy before any new president could impose his own will. The plan, like so many others during that session, was quickly discarded.

The Mississippi politician Jefferson Davis was elected temporary president of the new Confederacy. Rhett, despite his ambition, would not even be appointed to the administration. Ultimately, the man behind South Carolina's secession had to settle for a seat in the lower house of the Confederate Congress – hardly reward enough for all he'd done, Rhett thought. Things had not turned out the way he planned. In the coming years, Rhett would differ with Davis and the Congress often, using the *Mercury* to criticize the very Confederacy he had dreamed of creating.

His disappointment was evident from the start. On Feb. 23, 1861, the *Charleston Daily Courier* published its first edition under a banner that read, "Charleston, S.C., Confederate States of America." The *Mercury*, however, would never add "Confederate States" to its masthead.

Fort Sumter

CHAPTER 5

FORT SUMTER

Gunfire echoed through the streets of Charleston, rattling storefront windows as it rolled across the peninsula. The continuing volley – six, seven, eight shots – was followed by the unmistakable sounds of a large, screaming crowd. That afternoon it sounded as if war had finally come to the city.

The outburst may have startled some locals, but the 3,000 people who surrounded The Citadel Green on March 22, 1861, were nothing less than thrilled. So many people had turned out to see the Corps of Cadets' annual drill for the Board of Visitors that some were forced to watch from inside the barracks.

"Not an available window was there that did not exhibit a pair of rosy cheeks and laughing eyes, and the summit was alive with interested spectators," the *Mercury* reported. "Every South Carolinian is aware that the Cadets are the pride of the state."

The newspaper claimed the six companies on parade that day displayed so much skill in military discipline and maneuvering that they would compare favorably to the corps at West Point. It was a bold statement, and one that the man honored with the 11-gun salute was most qualified to judge.

Brig. Gen. Pierre Gustave Toutant Beauregard, the new commander at Charleston, had served briefly as superintendent of the U.S. Military Academy earlier in the year. After just five days on the job, his home state of Louisiana seceded and the U.S. War Department revoked Beauregard's orders – eliminating any question of whether he would remain loyal to the Union. The general resigned and joined the Confederate Army. Almost immediately, he was sent to South Carolina.

Beauregard watched the demonstration that afternoon while sitting among the school's professors and later, the *Mercury* reported, offered the corps a "high compliment." The cadets were delighted, but the general could have expected no less. Beauregard was quickly becoming accustomed to Charleston adulation – his arrival had prompted the city's largest celebration since the Secession Convention. And even though much of that was a reaction to Beauregard's larger-than-life reputation, it also hinted at the local morale. By the spring of 1861, Charleston was desperate for good news.

Aside from the formation of the Confederacy, the winter had seen little movement for the Southern cause. Uncertainty led to restlessness. Gov. Francis Pickens had been criticized widely, even in the South, for his treatment of the federal troops at Fort Sumter. He had tried to rehabilitate his image by sending the men fresh beef and vegetables in late January, a controversial attempt at public relations. Maj. Robert Anderson had politely declined the gift, but offered to come into the City Market and buy his own provisions. Pickens agreed to the arrangement, but Anderson never sent anyone into the city. Perhaps he thought better of it.

Pickens' generosity prompted a harsh rebuke from *Mercury* editor Robert Barnwell Rhett Jr., who demanded the state stop procrastinating and take Sumter immediately. The governor, in his reply, showed that he could be just as sarcastic and condescending with his own people as he was with Anderson. Pickens offered to furnish Rhett some men so that he could "storm the work" himself.

"But sir, I am not a military man," Rhett had said.

"Nor I either," the governor replied, "and therefore I take the advice of those who are."

After that, criticism of the governor abated considerably, and his remarks endeared him to state militia officers.

For all his impatience and willingness to send others into combat, Rhett spoke for a fair number of frustrated Charleston residents. Negotiations for the surrender of Fort Sumter had stalled in recent weeks, the United States unwilling to deal with the Confederate government for fear of legitimizing it. The *Mercury* ran a series of dispatches from New York papers that lamented the nation's predicament. The prevailing opinion seemed to be that giving up Sumter was the only way to avoid a war.

This tension permeated the city. Around Charleston, the newspaper reported, you could scarcely hear a conversation that did not include the words "Beauregard,

Confederate General P.G.T. Beauregard, commander at Charleston.

Anderson, Sumter, Moultrie and Morris Island." There were rumors that New York detectives had been sent to the city to watch for incoming ammunition, and speculation that the U.S. Army would blow up Sumter rather than surrender it. Beauregard's appointment to Charleston may have suggested that Confederate President Jefferson Davis feared the worst, but it was simply an acknowledgment of political reality. If there was going to be a war, the first shots would almost certainly be fired in Charleston.

The general shrewdly used public relations in an attempt to ease that local tension. On Saturday, March 30, Beauregard invited members of the State Convention and other distinguished guests to tour the harbor batteries by boat. He was eager to show off the progress his men had made in shoring up the city's defenses. The group gathered at Southern Wharf, where a color guard stood at attention while the Palmetto Band played "Dixie's Land," a minstrel song the South had recently adopted as its theme. From the wharf, the entourage set out on three steamers and was gone most of the day.

Mary Boykin Chesnut, wife of former U.S. Sen. James Chesnut, suggested in her famous diary that the general took undue credit for the military's work in the city. Just days before her husband was named Beauregard's aide-de-camp Mrs. Chesnut said the general was a "demigod" among Charlestonians. Some locals, however, noted that the major of engineers, William H.C. Whiting, did all the work while Beauregard reaped the glory.

No matter who deserved the credit, Beauregard's boat tour illustrated just how much the Southern troops had done. The group passed Fort Johnson and Fort Moultrie – both of which had been strengthened considerably – before sailing by Fort Sumter on the way into Maffitt's Channel. The guests had lunch as the boats drifted past Morris Island, where they noted considerable works, including the Iron Battery on Cummings Point. Sumter was almost completely surrounded by Confederate guns. As the tour ended that evening, those batteries fired a series of shots over the harbor.

"To a large majority of the spectators the flight and bursting of shell was something novel, and the scene was altogether grand and impressive," the *Mercury* reported.

It was exactly the sort of pomp and circumstance that Beauregard had requested, and it seemed to lift local spirits somewhat. But it would not last. The next time those batteries fired, it would not be for show.

On April 3 Beauregard and his aides gave Gov. Pickens a tour of Sullivan's Island batteries — perhaps another volley in the general's public relations campaign. After the group finished, they gathered on the porch of the Moultrie House hotel, where they soon noticed a schooner sailing toward the harbor. As it approached Morris Island, one of the batteries there fired a blank shot to warn off the unidentified vessel. In response, the ship raised a U.S. flag on its mast, which prompted three more shots – live ones, this time.

"A ship was fired into yesterday and went back to sea," Mary Chesnut wrote in her diary. "Is that the first shot? How can one settle down to anything? One's heart is in one's mouth all the time. Any minute, the cannon may open on us, the fleet come in."

Everyone in Charleston had a sense that after months of tedious waiting, war might come at any moment. Chesnut reflected the mood of many locals: The city seemed well prepared for conflict, if it came down to it, but who could predict what might happen? There was a sense that the entire country was watching, that history would be made within days.

Capt. Abner Doubleday later claimed that the jumpy Southerners had made a serious error that day. The *R.H. Shannon* was a civilian ship carrying a cargo of ice for Savannah that had wandered into the harbor to escape the fog offshore. When the first shot was fired, Doubleday said, the captain – hopelessly uninformed when it came to current events – raised the U.S. flag to show that he was a friend. When that prompted more firing, the captain lowered the flag and soon a boat from Morris Island set out to investigate.

As this unfolded, the men at Fort Sumter had their guns trained on the batteries, ready to fire – even though Doubleday conceded that Anderson likely would have shown restraint even if the ship were sunk right in front of them. That did not mean the Fort Sumter commander couldn't put up a good front. Soon after the incident, a boat from Sumter approached Morris Island flying a white flag of truce – and carrying words of warning.

The men delivered a note from Anderson that said, in essence, if the Confederates fired a shell that actually struck one of his ships he would unleash the full might of Sumter on the island batteries. It was brave talk from a man who was more desperate than ever.

Trapped inside the fort for three months, Anderson and his troops were running dangerously low on provisions – and there was no end in sight. In early April President Abraham Lincoln had sent word to Pickens that he planned to resupply the fort, a clear signal that he had no plans to relinquish Sumter. Lincoln told the governor that if he were allowed to deliver food to Anderson, he would make no attempts to reinforce Sumter with more troops. The Confederates would not agree to any such terms. The *Mercury* said the president's letter was practically a declaration of war.

Beauregard personally responded to Anderson's note that day. The two men were old friends – Anderson had been one of Beauregard's instructors at West Point. The two men thought highly of one another and, earlier in the year, had complimented each other publicly. Such was the nature of a civil war. Both men were astute enough military leaders to understand that their friendship had little to do with the situation, and each had to do what was right for his side. Beauregard's reply to Anderson said all attempts to deliver provisions to Sumter would be stopped by force. It was a stalemate.

Beauregard realized that he had the upper hand. He knew Sumter's stores were nearly exhausted, that the fort was still unfinished, and there was no chance to stock it — the Confederates had seen to that. The *Mercury* published a letter from a New York paper, reportedly from one of Anderson's men, which claimed there were four months of supplies remaining at Sumter. The *Mercury* – much as Beauregard did – discounted the report.

"The letter is probably a forgery, but, if it be genuine, the writer was either drunk or jesting," Rhett opined.

Throughout the first week of April, Charleston was quiet. There were rumors — there were always rumors — that a bombardment of the fort would commence at any minute, and that Anderson had fired upon a steamship attempting to enter the harbor. The *Mercury* dismissed these stories as being without any foundation. But it was clear that the endgame had begun.

"Things are happening so fast," Mary Chesnut wrote in her diary on April 8. "My husband has been made an aide-de-camp of General Beauregard. Three hours ago we were quietly packing to go home. The Convention had adjourned. Now he tells me the attack upon Fort Sumter may begin tonight."

As the second week of April 1861 began, the Confederates decided they must force Anderson out of Sumter before an attempt to restock the fort succeeded. The incident of the previous week – supply ship or not – served as a reminder that only one ship had to get through the defenses to extend this stalemate by months. And Beauregard could not allow that to happen. At 3 p.m. on Thursday, April 11, the general sent Col. Chesnut, Col. Chisolm and Capt. Stephen D. Lee to demand that Anderson's troops evacuate Sumter immediately.

He must have anticipated the response.

Anderson told the men he "could not, consistently with his honor as an officer of the United States Army, retire from his post without instructions from his government." But he told them not to waste their energy trying to force him out. Without provisions, Anderson said, he and his men would be starved out within days. It was an honest reply – so honest that some of his men assumed Anderson wanted to get out without a fight. But that answer, as candid as it may have been, was not good enough for the Confederates.

For the rest of the evening, Charleston waited with growing unease. A group of men gathered outside the *Mercury* offices to get the latest news — just as they had done on election night — but there was little to report until 11 p.m., when a bulletin suggested "the bombardment would not commence immediately."

"On the Battery several hundreds of persons, principally ladies, were promenading until near midnight, anxiously gazing at the dim lights, barely visible through the haze, which indicated the position of the batteries, where fathers and sons, brothers and lovers were willing to sacrifice their lives for the honor of South Carolina," the *Mercury* reported. "And yet there was but one regret expressed, and that was at the delay and procrastination of hostilities."

Mary Chesnut reported that her husband returned from Sumter that evening hungry and deeply troubled. Col. Chesnut, his wife said, "felt for Anderson" but had no choice but to follow the orders telegraphed into the city by Confederate President Jefferson Davis. And those orders sent Chesnut back to Sumter in the dead of night. After Chesnut left, his wife recorded his orders in her diary.

"I do not pretend to go to sleep," she wrote. "How can I? If Anderson does not accept terms at four o'clock, the orders are he shall be fired upon."

Chesnut and Lee delivered their latest scripted message to Sumter at 1:30 a.m. on April 12. They told Anderson the harbor batteries would not fire on the fort if no attempts were made to resupply it. But they could not give him provisions that might allow him to hold out long enough for "hostile plans" to mature. They asked when

Anderson would give up the fort peacefully, and he said perhaps April 15 – if he did not receive new orders. The Confederates did not like his answer, but had come to realize there were no terms agreeable to both sides. Negotiations were pointless. At 3:30 a.m., Beauregard sent his old friend one final message: In one hour's time, the batteries would open fire.

The South had declared war.

It was later described as a "splendid pyrotechnic exhibition."

At 4:30 a.m. on Friday, April 12, a battery just outside Fort Johnson on James Island fired a shell that arced over the harbor in a "beautiful curve" before bursting immediately over Fort Sumter. Later, some would claim the famous secessionist and fire-eater Edmund Ruffin was given the honor of firing the first shot of the war. Doubleday himself would credit Ruffin, arguing that the shot from Fort Johnson was merely a signal to other batteries, and that the fire-eater had fired the first direct shot at Sumter from Cummings Point. Nevertheless, the man who fired the shot from James Island – Capt. George Sholter James of the South Carolina Artillery – was ultimately credited with firing the first shot of the American Civil War.

Within 15 minutes of that first burst, other batteries from around the harbor joined in the bombardment. Mary Chesnut wrote that she had been awake to count four chimes from the St. Michael's bell and, a half-hour later, heard the first cannon. "I sprang out of bed and on my knees, prostrate, I prayed as I never prayed before," she wrote.

The rolling thunder of continued fire drew hundreds of Charlestonians out of bed as well. Instead of praying, however, many quickly made their way to The Battery, where they watched two hours of Southern shooting go unanswered by Fort Sumter.

"While the early sun was veiled in mist, we saw shell bursting within and illuminating Fort Sumter, or exploding in the air above, leaving a small thick cloud of white smoke to mark the place," the *Mercury* reported. "We saw solid shot striking the dark walls, and in each instance followed by a fume of dust from the battered surface."

Inside Fort Sumter, the federal troops were calm in the face of attack. Doubleday later reported that some were "even somewhat merry." The officers had a breakfast of pork and water while they waited for daylight to return fire. Anderson wanted to see his targets in order to preserve supplies. Sumter had thousands of pounds of

The bombardment of Fort Sumter.

powder and a sizeable stockpile of projectiles, but the fort was low on cartridge bags which held the powder for the cannons. His men had worked desperately to build up a supply of the bags with any cloth available to them, but they had only one needle to sew the bags. It was slow work, but they had no other choice.

About 7 a.m., Fort Sumter fought back. Doubleday fired the first gun in defense of the Union – a shot aimed at the Iron Battery on Cummings Point. He later said he had "no feeling of self-reproach, for I fully believed the contest was inevitable, and was not of our seeking." The shot bounced off the battery's sloping roof without any "apparent effect."

Anderson quickly turned his guns toward Fort Moultrie, Fort Johnson and a floating battery off Sullivan's Island. The two sides continued the barrage for hours,

Fort Sumter fights back.

mortar shells shaking Sumter's parade ground like an earthquake, the sound of cannon fire echoing across the harbor.

"Hour after hour has the fire on both sides been kept up, deliberate and unflagging," the *Mercury* reported. "The steady, frequent shock of the cannon's boom, accompanied by the hiss of balls, and the horrid, hurtling sound of the flying shell, are now perfectly familiar to the people of Charleston."

From the start, it appeared that the Southerners were getting the best of the battle; Beauregard was pleased with the reports he got from his men. These updates poured in throughout the day, each more encouraging than the last.

"The balls from Fort Sumter are doing little or no damage, not one person having been injured," Fort Moultrie reported that afternoon.

Fort Johnson sent word that "Anderson has fired two shots, but without effect."

Morris Island relayed the news that "two of the guns on the iron battery have been partially disabled, but no one injured."

By afternoon, those guns had been repaired and resumed firing. The battery commanders estimated that four out of every six shots fired fell inside Sumter. These projectiles were doing damage, too. The fort's barracks caught fire several times, distracting the troops who rushed to extinguish the flames.

Despite the barrage, the men of Fort Sumter kept a sense of humor. After three hours of non-stop shooting, Doubleday's men were relieved by Capt. Seymour's detachment. According to the following exchange from Doubleday's book, the captain seemed in light spirits, given the intensity of the battle.

"Doubleday," Seymour said, "what in the world is the matter here, and what is all this uproar about?"

"There's a trifling difference of opinion between us and our neighbors opposite," Doubleday replied, playing along, "and we are trying to settle it."

The bombardment ended at dark on Friday, but began again in earnest at first light on Saturday. Again, Sumter was slow to return fire. Most of Anderson's guns were trained on Fort Moultrie, one of the closest and biggest targets. The *Mercury*, which declared Moultrie "impregnable," reported that the fort withstood the fire admirably.

"The quarters were knocked to hell, but nobody hurt," one officer reported to the paper.

At 8 a.m. locals spotted a plume of thick, black smoke coming from the southern part of Sumter's barracks. Soon, flames were visible to troops on shore. The Confederates kept firing and by midday much of the fort was enveloped in black smoke. And then, early that afternoon, the U.S. flag went down. For most of the morning it had been hanging by a single halyard, the rigging damaged by a shell. The shot at 12:48 p.m., reportedly fired by Lt. W.C. Preston of South Carolina, finished the job.

When the flag fell, the troops on Morris Island moved quickly. Col. L.T. Wigfall and Pvt. H. Gourdin Young of the Palmetto Guard boarded a small boat and had slaves carry them across the shallows to Sumter. Wigfall held his sword high in the air with a white handkerchief tied to it. It was a dangerous trip — the Sullivan's Island batteries had spotted the U.S. flag rise out of the smoke and resumed firing. Somehow, Wigfall's boat managed to reach the Sumter wharf without being struck.

The colonel walked into the fort, called out for Anderson and explained the situation. The fort was under distress and no flag was flying, so he had come to negotiate Sumter's surrender. Wigfall was acting without Beauregard's blessing, some later claimed, and did not have the authority to set such terms. But the Confederates didn't protest too much. Beauregard was consulted after the fact, and he agreed to abide by the terms Wigfall had set out.

Col. L.T. Wigfall negotiates the surrender with Col. Anderson.

Anderson was in little position to argue. He was low on supplies and realized he could not repel an attack that came from all sides at once, not with his limited resources. The fort had been unable to use all its guns because Anderson wouldn't allow his men to put themselves in harm's way by firing from unprotected parts of the fort. Stuck in the lower levels of the fort, his men were miserable. At times the smoke had been so bad that they had to lie down and put their mouths on the ground just to breathe. Anderson realized he could not continue, and agreed to surrender the fort the next day.

The first battle of the Civil War was over.

The transfer of Fort Sumter would not pass without some ceremony. Anderson's one demand was that he be allowed to honor the U.S. flag with a gun salute as it was lowered. Pickens and Beauregard and his officers all would observe the historic event, boarding a steamer at Southern Wharf for the short trip to the fort. And there, they would witness the first casualty of the war.

About midway through the 100-gun salute, the *Mercury* reported, there was an errant explosion — an ember left burning in one of the guns prematurely ignited the powder in it. U.S. Army Pvt. Daniel Hough was killed almost instantly, and several other troops were injured, one of whom would die later. The gun salute was capped at 50 shots as a result, and the private was buried on the parade grounds. After 30-plus hours of fighting, Hough was the first man to die in the Civil War.

After the salute, the Palmetto Guard entered the fort, reportedly bringing secessionist Edmund Ruffin with them. One excited soldier mistakenly raised the banner of the Palmetto Guard over Sumter before the Stars and Bars of the Confederacy was hoisted. Finally, the state flag of South Carolina went up. And with that, the South finally had control of Fort Sumter.

Anderson and his men were allowed to leave Charleston and exited the fort to the tune of "Yankee Doodle" – it seemed the North had its own theme song. Doubleday, with the permission of Anderson, had walked out early, while the U.S. flag was still flying. He was outside the fort's walls when he heard the thunderous applause of Southerners saluting the flags that replaced it.

The federal troops boarded the *Isabel* to sail out of Charleston, but they lingered at the fort too long and the tides left them stranded until the next morning. They were forced to sit outside Sumter all night, listening to the men celebrate under the first Confederate flag to fly over Fort Sumter.

The South had won the first round, but there seemed little chance it would be the last. On Monday, April 15, the Charleston *Mercury* carried a simple headline: "Lincoln Declares War."

The Palmetto Guard marches down Meeting Street.

CHAPTER 6

DIXIE LAND

The parade began under a threatening sky. A battalion of State Cadets escorted the men of the Palmetto Guard through downtown Charleston, the group marching in tight formation down Meeting Street on the way to Institute Hall. The procession stirred such excitement that not even the foreboding weather could dissuade the ladies of the city – "especially the young ladies," the *Mercury* reported – from turning out en masse for the second celebration of the Guard's heroics in less than a week.

The companies quietly filed inside the grand hall, drawing up close to the stage as the officers took their seats on the platform, where they joined members of the governor's staff and the commanders of at least two rifle regiments. After a brief selection by the band, the Guard was presented with a blue silk flag fringed with gold tassels. The banner, sporting a palmetto and the Guard's motto, was a gift from the women of Charleston in appreciation of their heroics at the battle of Fort Sumter.

When Lt. Col. Wilmot G. DeSaussure of the South Carolina Artillery presented the flag to Capt. George Cuthbert, he urged the Guard to "make their future deeds worthy of their glorious past."

That glorious past would scarcely be forgotten anytime soon. In the three weeks since the battle, there had been little talk in Charleston that did not focus on the victory at Fort Sumter. The prior Thursday, the Guard had been presented with a massive gold medal in a ceremony attended by Gen. Beauregard and the governor at the same venue. The ladies had decided to present the Guard with the new banner on this day, May 6, 1861, because of persistent rumors that the men soon would be sent off to fight in the war.

For all the talk that the Fort Sumter battle had signaled the start of a war, little had happened since. No further skirmishes had erupted, and Charleston had not heard a single gun fired in battle since April 13. Still, the gossip was as ceaseless as the tides, as contradictory as it was disturbing. The *Mercury* reprinted articles from Northern newspapers that suggested the United States was already plotting to retake the fort and all the other federal property seized by the Confederates in Charleston.

Gen. Winfield Scott said, according to a dispatch from Richmond, that the U.S. Army "would not march an army of invasion into any of the seceded States, but that they would retake Forts Moultrie, Sumter and Harper's Ferry at any cost."

The *Mercury* stirred partisan rancor locally by reprinting the New York *Tribune*'s summary of the battle at Sumter. The piece referred to Southerners as "seceders" who would soon be forced to "abandon their great conspiracy." Robert Barnwell Rhett Jr. could not have chosen a better editorial to rouse Charlestonians into frenzy.

"We mean to conquer them — not merely defeat, but to conquer, to SUBJUGATE them — and we will do this the most mercifully, the more speedily we do it," the *Tribune* opined, according to the *Mercury*.

Rhett tried to keep spirits high in Charleston by claiming in the *Mercury* that "God is with us," that "He will support the truth, the right, the pure, the just." Their enemies – primarily Northern politicians – would be punished for the crime of attempting to inflict their will on the Southern people.

"By tariffs, navigation laws, internal improvements, and infernal appropriations, they swallowed up all our revenues," Rhett wrote. "In their vanity and pride of heart they mocked at God — forgot Him — mocked at us — and now seek to destroy us."

For readers unimpressed by claims of divine intervention, the editor offered more secular fare, reprinting the lyrics of "Dixie's Land" with new stanzas created especially for the Confederacy. Among them:

I suppose you've heard the awful news,

Of Lincoln and his kangaroos.

Fight away, fight away, fight away Dixie Land.

The more cynical readers of the *Mercury* might have been less cheered by another new verse that began, "We have no ships, we have no navies / But mighty faith in great Jeff Davis." It seemed an ominous sign that week when a fishing boat christened *Dixie* capsized in the harbor, killing two fishermen – an incident the newspaper referred to briefly as a "melancholy casualty."

More local matters dominated the news as the glory of Sumter faded from the pages nearly a month after the battle. On May 24 a slave got into a gunfight with the local militia. A guard had spotted Anthony — "belonging to the estate of J.C. Beamann," the *Mercury* reported — out late without a pass near the intersection of Meeting and Chalmers. When one officer tried to arrest Anthony, he fought back and eventually pulled a pistol. The slave managed to fire three shots before he was subdued. No one was injured, but the next week a local court sentenced Anthony to six months solitary imprisonment and "twenty paddles on the first day of each month."

By the time Anthony finished serving his sentence, he would find Charleston forever changed.

Officially, there was no conflict.

The U.S. Congress and President Abraham Lincoln refused to formally declare war on the Confederate States. Washington officials argued that the United States made such proclamations only against recognized nations, and neither Lincoln nor the Congress would dignify the Confederacy with such status – an insult to the Southerners. To the North this was only a rebellion, and nothing more. The Confederate Congress did not quibble with such details, passing a declaration of war in Montgomery just before the Southern government moved its capital to Richmond, Va.

Even if the United States did not officially consider itself at war, Lincoln was nonetheless preparing a military buildup. After the battle at Fort Sumter and some trouble in other states, the president called for 75,000 volunteer troops – asking the men to enlist for three-month tours. That, Lincoln thought, would be long enough to retake all the federal forts and restore the Union. But his order would have unintended consequences. Lincoln's call for additional troops only escalated tensions in the country.

Four Southern states that had initially resisted the Confederacy's overtures — Virginia, Arkansas, Tennessee and North Carolina — chose to secede rather than supply troops to fight their neighbors. As one new verse in "Dixie Land" noted, "The Southern States were only seven / But we've got 'em up now to eleven." The United States was quickly falling apart, and the First National flag of the Confederacy flying at Fort Sumter would need additional stars.

Virginia not only provided the Confederacy with a new capital, it quickly became the nexus of the conflict as Northern and Southern troops converged there to intercept one another. There were a few skirmishes, but nothing approaching a full battle until June 10 in Bethel Church, a small town on Chesapeake Bay. The *Mercury* reported that even though the Southern troops were outnumbered three-to-one, they still claimed an easy victory.

"The enemy were so completely and effectually repulsed, that they are unable to put any other face on the result, and are forced to confess their defeat, route and pursuit into the very streets of Hampton," Rhett claimed.

By the time this news reached Charleston, the Palmetto Guard was on its way north.

Three days after the Palmetto Guard was feted at Institute Hall, they were on parade yet again. The occasion this time was far less celebratory, although that was not evident in the reaction of Charleston residents. The Guard was "accompanied by at least a thousand friends, a very large proportion of whom were ladies," as they set out from the Adamesque-style South Carolina Society Hall at 9 that night.

The Guard marched up Meeting Street, stopping briefly at Military Hall on Wentworth Street, where they were joined by escorts from the Corps of Cadets and the Carolina Light Infantry. The procession then moved north to John Street and the Northeastern Railroad Depot. And there the city said farewell to the Palmetto Guard. An "immense concourse had assembled to bid the Palmettos good-byes," the *Mercury* reported, with ladies waving their handkerchiefs as a band played strains of martial music. When the men lined up next to their train cars, someone proposed three cheers for Cuthbert, the Guard's commander. Three more followed for their safe return.

And then they were gone, the *Mercury* reported the next day, "off to defend the soil of the Old Dominion."

Like U.S. officials, the Confederates thought the war would be a short one – but for different reasons. After their successes at Fort Sumter and Bethel Church, the Southerners expected to make quick work of the Union Army. They had the enthusiasm, the bravado and, they believed they were on the right side of history. Still, they would not make the mistake of over-confidence. As Union forces moved into Virginia, the Confederate Army sent many of its best resources to intercept the Yankees, including Beauregard. With the general and the Palmetto Guard out of town, Charleston suddenly felt much quieter.

As the summer began, the city tensely awaited news from the front. Many feared the Union would attempt to retake Sumter at any moment. The appearance of a sloop offshore prompted speculation that the Yankees were on a reconnaissance mission. And when cannon fire echoed across the harbor in the early morning of June 18, some feared Lincoln had sent ships to bombard Sumter. A few even got dressed, ran into the streets and down to the wharves to make sure they didn't miss the action.

"One young gentleman, who must have been laboring under terrible excitement, assured his friends he had seen shells thrown from Stono, and that a most damaging fire had been kept up at Sumter and Moultrie," the *Mercury* reported.

As it turned out, the firing was only a test of the local garrisons.

The next round of shelling came on July 4, and some Charleston residents assumed the forts were celebrating Independence Day. A salute was even fired from the city, which had suspended most business. But the following day, local military leaders quickly quashed the speculation, saying that they "positively declined to offer any such salute."

"These officers stated that on the 28th of June (the anniversary of Fort Moultrie's Revolutionary victory against the British Navy), however, they did not wait for orders to salute; and on the 20th of December next they shall not wait for orders," the *Mercury* reported.

The newspaper endorsed the stance of these local military leaders, suggesting that "Independence Day" would, in fact, be more properly celebrated now on the anniversary of South Carolina's secession.

On Friday, July 19, the *Mercury* reported that "the long-expected conflict between the forces of Beauregard and McDowell has begun" in Virginia. Actually, the real fighting was two days away, but that was only a technicality. The battle was called Bull Run by Union troops and Manassas by the Southerners. And it quickly disavowed both sides of any preconceived notions of a short war.

It was a messy battle. Beauregard and Brig. Gen. Irvin McDowell initially, and unsuccessfully, tried to outflank each other before finally falling into a clumsy fight. At first the U.S. troops held the upper hand, but when Confederate reinforcements arrived the momentum shifted. Spectators from Washington, who picnicked on the outskirts of the battlefield, got more of a show than they expected. In the bloody fight, the South lost 387 men; the North suffered 460 deaths. Both sides limped away with more than 1,000 wounded. But the South had won again.

The *Mercury* would print a dozen or more accounts of the battle — including some from Northern newspapers — and proudly proclaimed that "a battle such as the New World had never yet beheld, has been fought at Manassas." In an ode to Beauregard published a week after the battle, Rhett went so far as to call it "the most stupendous battle ever fought upon the Western Hemisphere." All that hyperbole aside, the news that Charleston residents awaited most nervously came days earlier, on July 24. The *Mercury* reported that the city's first casualties from the battle would arrive at the train station that morning.

"A squadron of mounted troops will receive the remains at the Northeastern railroad depot this morning, and escort them to City Hall, which has been draped in mourning for their reception," the paper said. "The remains of the deceased will lie in state for some hours, to enable our citizens to pay their last visit of respect."

The names of local men killed at Manassas trickled out over the next several days — W.D. Porter, A.F. Ravenel, T.L. Hutchison and W.F. Colcock among them. Local troops marched the bodies of Gen. Bernard Bee and Lt. Col. Benjamin J. Johnson from City Hall to St. Paul's Church. Such ceremonies would soon become all too common in the city.

In the midst of these funerals, the fight briefly returned to Charleston. On July 28 a privateer christened *Petrel* was sunk offshore as it was attempting to leave the harbor. For months, local residents worried that the U.S. Navy would try to block-ade Charleston Harbor. There were rumors that several U.S.-flagged ships had been spotted offshore, but no confirmation of those reports was made until the attack on the *Petrel*. The ship was a U.S. revenue cutter, the *Aiken*, which had been seized after the secession vote. Re-christened and refitted by a group of local businessmen, it had taken months to prepare the ship for its initial cruise. But the new owners made one fatal mistake: They equipped the *Petrel* with only two guns. The U.S. frigate *St. Lawrence*, by contrast, carried 52 guns.

The *Petrel* snuck out of the harbor on the night of July 27 and spotted the *St. Lawrence* offshore at dawn the next morning. Unable to outrun the warship, the *Petrel*'s

The Battle of Manassas

crew did the only thing that came to mind: they raised a Confederate flag and fired on the frigate. The *Petrel* got off one good shot, hitting the frigate's mainsail, before the *St. Lawrence*'s crew returned fire. Within minutes, the Navy ship landed a shot on the *Petrel*'s bow that ended the skirmish. Four members of the privateer's crew drowned and the rest were rescued by the *St. Lawrence* and carried to Philadelphia, where they would stand trial.

The news had greater implication for locals: It seemed the U.S. Navy was indeed conducting an unofficial blockade of the port. Between this realization and the mounting number of funerals for the Manassas casualties, the realities of war were quickly coming to Charleston.

The bombardment of Port Royal.

CHAPTER 7

BATTLE ROYAL

A hoarse thunder disrupted the still of a "glorious autumn morn" in Charleston, a rumbling noise that sent hundreds running toward The Battery. It was an eruption similar to the report of guns that announced the bombardment of Fort Sumter seven months earlier and residents – fearing a Yankee attack – hurried to see what the war had brought on this day.

An intense excitement permeated the air for several minutes, until all the gawkers reached the waterfront and saw nothing on the horizon except calm forts. The crowds quickly dispersed, although they would talk about little else for the rest of the day. A few of the more worried and curious made their way to the *Mercury* offices on Broad Street to await the news. A series of telegrams delivered updates throughout the day, each bearing successively bad news. On Thursday morning, Nov. 7, 1861, South Carolina was on the verge of changing irrevocably.

The gunfire was "no hoax, but grim reality," the paper reported the next day. Those shots, plainly audible in the city, announced "the long expected demonstration by the enemy's naval expedition." In fact, the noise that startled Charleston that morning carried up the coast about 50 miles. In Beaufort County, Port Royal was under attack.

Since Fort Sumter, no significant battles had yet occurred in South Carolina. The fight had moved west and into Virginia. Charleston residents had been relegated to the sidelines after witnessing the start of the war. The *Mercury* kept locals informed of the daily happenings in the War Between the States, but all of it was occurring elsewhere. Every day, the paper printed dispatches from "the war in Missouri" or "the war in Kentucky," where Confederate troops were trying to keep Union forces out of Tennessee.

Since Manassas, Charleston's most direct role in recent events was holding 100 prisoners of war from the battle. The Yankee soldiers were shipped in by train and jailed at Castle Pinckney. Later some were moved to the City Jail, an event that prompted headlines in the *Mercury* for days. Such was the tedium of life as a spectator to war. Several Dahlgren guns had been shipped in to aid in the city's defenses, eliciting more glowing news, but some locals wondered if they would ever see action.

Some tried to rekindle the patriotic atmosphere of the spring by using the German Volunteers' departure for Virginia as an excuse to throw an elaborate party. On Tuesday, Sept. 10, the men were served a substantial dinner at the Pavilion Hotel. Then, at noon, the company marched down Meeting Street, escorted by the Palmetto Riflemen and German Artillery, to Institute Hall. There, the *Mercury* reported, "the galleries and sides of the Hall were thronged with ladies, and when company after company of the stalwart Teutons had filed into their places in front of the stage, the room presented a very pleasant and inspiriting scene."

Such celebration was rare for Charleston in the fall of 1861. For the most part, less cheerful events dominated the city's attention. Authorities had detained several slaves for illegally selling produce on the docks. Then a 12-year-old slave boy apparently committed suicide by lying on railroad tracks until a train came through. But the most shocking news came in mid-September when four slaves tried to poison their mistress at her home on Vanderhorst Street. Prompt medical attention saved the woman's life, but her servants got no such reprieve. Little more than a month later, they were executed.

And then there was the case of the mysterious man who called himself Rothschild, a name that conjured suggestions of high finance and banking empires. The man had checked into the Charleston Hotel in mid-September and immediately caught the eye of locals. Many thought the gentleman with the exotic name acted suspiciously. When this Rothschild suddenly changed his travel plans and left the city in a hurry, he was tracked to Savannah. There, he immediately caught another train back to Charleston, where he was eventually detained for questioning. The *Mercury* reported that Rothschild was carrying a valise "filled with gold, and his trunk, which is at the Lower Guard House, is rather too heavy for clothing."

The man was merely a merchant from Charlotte. He shipped many of his goods to Charleston and converted the stock to gold — about $8,000 worth. He was ultimately released, but still eyed warily. Such events consumed Charleston in the fall of 1861, until the Union attacked the South Carolina coast.

The attack on Port Royal should not have been a surprise.

Throughout the summer and into the fall, the city watched as hostile ships sailed over the horizon and half-heartedly tried to blockade Charleston Harbor. Some of them would linger for days, perhaps even prevent a few ships from leaving port before sailing away. Many of those ships carried native Southerners who had been forced to choose between their home and their profession.

In Charleston, the Middleton family suddenly had to confront the notion that they might have to take up arms against their own blood. Edward Middleton, younger brother of Ordinance of Secession signers Williams and John Middleton, was a captain in the U.S. Navy when the war began. While his brothers were fiercely Southern, Edward felt duty-bound to his country. In 1861 Edward Middleton tried to explain the dilemma to his confused family.

"I hold that in times of revolution an officer bound by his oath is not at liberty to throw off his allegiance and serve against his late government," Edward wrote, "even if he should be so disposed."

For much of the year, the Middleton brothers would expend much time and effort trying to convince Edward to come home – that his place was with his family, not at sea. Edward's protests held no sway over his brothers so he turned to his sister, Eliza. He lamented that, "These views of mine may be regarded in some quarters now as unsound, but the time may come when they will be admitted to be consistent with (the) principles (of) ... all honorable men."

The fact that Edward's own Navy was bearing down on Charleston only made matters worse for the Middleton family. Gen. Winfield Scott was still developing his "Anaconda Plan" to choke the South by shutting down its ports and already the ships were beginning to arrive, prompting a major shift in the war. The Union discovered that, on the water, it held a decided advantage.

In late August, seven Union Navy ships had attacked two Confederate forts on the Outer Banks of North Carolina. The ships bombarded Fort Hatteras and Fort Clark for two days before the Southern troops, outgunned and overpowered, surrendered. The *Mercury* spent the early part of September fretting over "the fall of Fort Hatteras," and for good reason: It was the first significant Union victory of the war. Taking those Outer Banks forts gave the federals a little confidence after their failure at Bull Run, and some political cover to continue fighting. And it led to a new plan of attack.

After the battle at Hatteras Inlet, South Carolina should have realized that it was next. It seemed the Union now possessed a solid formula for success, and there was no better place to test this than the state where the war began, where the politicians in Washington were desperate to strike a killing blow. The state had three tempting targets for such an assault: the port of Georgetown, Charleston Harbor and Port Royal Sound. And it was clear which would be most easily penetrated.

Beauregard quickly recognized that Port Royal was the coast's most vulnerable spot. But when he told South Carolina officials that the mouth of the sound was too wide to defend simply with forts on either side of its entrance, he was ignored. Instead, the Confederates built defenses on Hilton Head Island, on the southern side of the sound, and on St. Phillips Island to the north. St. Phillips sat just behind Fripp Island, three miles or so north of Hilton Head. The water between those batteries was wide enough to sail a fleet through. If that weren't bad enough, as of November 1861 neither fort was finished.

Despite Beauregard's warnings, South Carolinians were not overly alarmed when, on Nov. 2, a correspondent for the *Mercury* reported that "a Great Yankee Armada" was allegedly sailing down the coast. It was thought, the newspaper assured Charleston, that these Union ships were headed for "Savannah or Brunswick, Georgia."

For the first few days of November, dreary weather battered Charleston and churned the harbor into a heavy chop. At the same time, a fleet of more than a dozen warships and several other assorted vessels trudged through the same system as they made their way down the East Coast. Flag Officer Samuel Francis du Pont, the 58-year-old leader of the convoy, meant to repeat the victorious strategy used at Hatteras Inlet on Port Royal Sound. But the weather was forcing considerable delays on his fleet, which some considered the largest ever assembled. The storms ultimately forced some ships to leave the convoy. A few even sank. Conditions were so bad that by the time du Pont's fleet reached the South Carolina coast, his options for attack

The gun "Jeff Davis," in Port Royal, South Carolina. The Confederates did not have nearly enough large guns to repel the Union Navy when it invaded Port Royal Sound in November of 1861. Library of Congress photo

were significantly diminished.

He had been extremely cautious about revealing his target, giving most captains their orders – and even their destination – in sealed envelopes that they could open only after they were at sea. Still Northern newspapers got word of du Pont's target and reported on the attack before it actually occurred. Those stories, which listed South Carolina as the fleet's destination, ran in the Charleston papers on Nov. 3. But it would be three days later before the *Mercury* reported the attack on Hilton Head Island.

By the time that story made the paper, it was all over.

"The enemy's fleet engaged our batteries for forty-five minutes at ebb tide to-day, and they have gone out of range," the paper announced. "One steamer was hit with a ball, and towed off. Another large steamer is aground since yesterday. Thirty-three vessels are now in sight."

The Confederates thought du Pont intended to land his troops on Hilton Head Island and storm the defenses on foot. But Capt. F. Peck of the steamer *Cecile* told the *Mercury* such a plan of attack was entirely dependent on calm seas. And du Pont did not have that luxury. The sea was restless on the morning of Nov. 7 as du Pont began his run at the mouth of Port Royal Sound. He sent 10 boats in with orders to shoot while moving, which would make it harder for the forts to return fire. It was the same strategy employed at Hatteras, and it produced similar results.

The firefight continued for hours. Many of the shells from Fort Walker (on Hilton Head) and Fort Beauregard (on St. Phillips) missed the moving targets, enough that du Pont's men were able to advance into the sound. The next day, Charleston learned details of the engagement from refugees who had fled Hilton Head Island during the shooting.

"The steamer *Savannah* arrived here at 6 p.m., having been struck three times, but sustaining no serious injury," the *Mercury* reported. "She reports that 15 vessels had passed the batteries at Port Royal up to 12 o'clock. Walker's battery is doing good work. Several of the Yankee fleet have been crippled."

That good work would not be enough to repel the Yankee horde for long. By early afternoon, the Confederates were running out of ammunition in their unfinished forts, the ones that Beauregard had warned South Carolina were too little, too late.

The Confederates at Fort Walker never really had a chance.

The new fort was designed to hold seven 10-inch Columbiad cannons on its sea face, but when the soldiers arrived to man Walker they discovered that they had only one of the big guns. The rest were light cannons that were of little use against a fleet of warships. Also, someone delivered the wrong size of ammunition for the guns, which severely cut down on their stocks. The final insult came early in the battle. After firing less than a half-dozen shots, the one powerful Columbiad the troops had was damaged.

After a morning of heavy shelling, Brig. Gen. Thomas F. Drayton realized his gunners were so fatigued that he left the fort and returned with men from another battery to replace them. But by early afternoon they were low on ammunition, and only three of the guns on the seaward wall were still firing. And the Union ships kept coming. It was time to retreat.

Just after 2 p.m., Union sailors spied several Confederates leaving Fort Walker and sent a boat ashore to negotiate terms of surrender. They found Walker abandoned. The ease with which the Union sailors took control of the fort set off a chain reaction that basically ended the fight. When the Yankees raised the American flag over the Hilton Head Island fort, the Confederates on St. Phillips abandoned their position before ground troops could trap them on the island. Soon, the Union held Fort Beauregard as well as Walker.

In little more than half a day, the Union military claimed a most strategic piece of the South Carolina coast. Unaware of this outcome, Robert Barnwell Rhett Jr. opined in the Nov. 8 edition of the *Mercury* that the battle was destined to occur and predicted an altogether different outcome. "South Carolina began the war; and it is, perhaps, fitting, in the nature of things, that she should end it. The rage and hate of her enemies have precipitated them on her coast. They come to punish her, for daring to assert her liberties and independence."

Still, Rhett knew better than to assume a Southern victory, and he also realized that a Union presence at Hilton Head Island held serious consequences for Charleston. If the Yankees made it onto South Carolina soil, the city would be in great danger. That is most likely why he tried to inspire the patriotism rampant in the city during the first half of the year.

"If they can take Charleston, with twenty-five thousand men, let them have it," Rhett wrote. "We are unworthy to possess it; and it will be a fitting memorial — laid in ashes — of our imbecility and degeneracy. But if, on the contrary, we shall give to every one of our invaders, who shall remain on our soil, a prison above it or a grave beneath it — will it not end the contest?"

They were hopeful, defiant words from a city that held the ironic attitude that, "It is better for South Carolina to be the cemetery of freemen, than the home of slaves." By the time Rhett's pep talk was distributed throughout Charleston, Union forces were well on their way to occupying St. Helena Island, Beaufort and much of the land just north of the city. From there, U.S. troops would have little resistance as they marched north. Soon, the Yankees truly would be in Charleston's back yard, bringing the fight full circle back to the city where it began.

The days of reading about the war from afar were over.

The Roman Catholic Cathedral of St. John and St. Finbar, located on the corner of Broad and Legare streets, was one of the last major public buildings to fall in the final hours of the Great Fire of 1861.

CHAPTER 8

FIRE

John Raven Matthewes saw the men before they reached the plantation. They were moving at a leisurely pace across the island but stepped with the understated precision and formation of a military unit – which they were. They carried rifles and their uniforms were dark blue, almost black. Yankees.

When Matthewes realized this, he knew what he must do.

Since taking Port Royal Sound earlier in the month, the Union had landed thousands of soldiers on South Carolina soil. These troops were now inching their way north toward Charleston, but so far had little to show for their invasion. The soldiers found Beaufort deserted, drafted slaves into military service on Hilton Head and by Nov. 27 were beginning to infiltrate the islands around Edisto. That day, they reached Matthewes' plantation on Bear Island, east of Green Pond.

Matthewes realized why they had come, what they wanted. He was one of the most successful rice and cotton planters in the Lowcountry, and it had been a very good year for his crops. But, Matthewes later said, he was not about to let a bunch of Lincolnites use his land as a supply depot. Although it broke his heart, Matthewes did not hesitate – he set fire to his fields. He watched the flames for a moment and then turned to his house with resignation in his eyes. It would have to go too; Matthewes couldn't bear for his home to provide shelter for enemy soldiers.

Just as he was about to light a match to his home, the cavalry arrived — literally. Confederate troops stumbled onto the scene and forced the Yanks to retreat, allowing the South to hold Bear Island and Green Pond near the Combahee River, at least for the moment. Matthewes was so heartened that he turned his home over as a place for the Southern troops to quarter. He felt it was the least he could do.

The scene at Bear Island was not unusual; similar incidents played out across the Lowcountry in the fall of 1861 — the results not always so good for locals. The *Mercury* reported that Edward Baynard had burned his cotton fields and Edisto Island home to keep them from falling into Union hands. Within days, the Confederate military arrived and burned every cotton field on the island. There would be no crops to "gladden the hearts of the Yankee marauders," the *Mercury* reported. Robert Barnwell Rhett Jr. held great regard for these patriotic Southerners.

"Such noble sacrifices to the cause of the South deserve the highest praise," Rhett wrote.

As the anniversary of secession approached, there was little else to lift spirits in Charleston. The fall of 1861 had been plagued with bad news. Southern privateers were being intercepted at sea, their crews tried as pirates. Union ships were even making advances on Rockville, at the southern end of Wadmalaw Island, creeping ever closer to the city. Now Edisto was in ruins. To some, it seemed only a matter of time before Yankees marched onto the peninsula.

"On South Carolina, especially, the hate and fury of our enemies are turned," Rhett wrote in the *Mercury* on Dec. 9. "To ravage and burn down our beautiful city, and to crush our every particle of that free spirit which has given our State an honorable renown, will be their earnest effort."

Not even the arrival of Gen. Robert E. Lee, who checked into the Mills House for a planned tour of the city's harbor defenses, did much to raise local morale. Most of the city was in a foul mood. But as a cold winter wind blew across the peninsula, Charleston residents were about to learn that things could get even worse.

No one would ever know for sure how the fire started.

The alarm sounded at 8:30 on the night of Dec. 11, and some people claimed that the fire seemed to appear in three places simultaneously. The *Mercury* reported that the blaze began at Russell and Co.'s Sash and Blind factory, a three-story wooden building at the foot of Hasell Street near the Cooper River. But others maintained it was burning just as early on the south side of the street at Cameron and Co.'s Immense Machine Shops. Rhett never specified the third locale named as the fire's origin, which only fanned the flames of conspiracy.

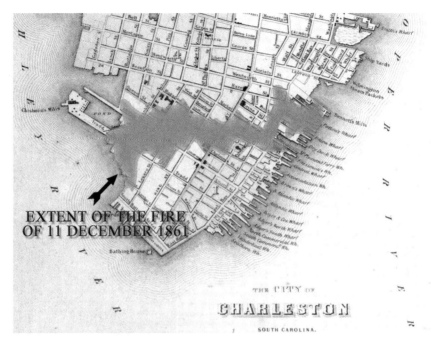

EXTENT OF THE FIRE
OF 11 DECEMBER 1861

This map shows the path of the fire super-imposed on a 19th century map of the city. Image courtesy of the Charleston Museum.

In later years many Charlestonians alternately blamed Union sympathizers or slaves, who were pegged as arsonists anytime there was a mysterious fire in the city. But in a note written years after the war, Fire Chief Moses Henry Nathan said simply that the "carelessness" of workers at Russell and Co.'s factory sparked the disaster. The owner, Nathan wrote, allowed "debris from the upper floor to be carried to the lower floor near the furnace" and did not have a "proper watchman on his premises."

"On several occasions previous the premises were on fire before and put out by the workmen of Cameron and Co. opposite," Nathan noted.

At the time, however, no one had time to assign blame. The Palmetto Fire Engine Company, a volunteer team stationed on Anson Street, rushed to the scene but did not have enough hose to reach the flames. Other companies soon arrived but found they had more serious issues. The blaze began at dead low tide, leaving the team without enough water to smother the flames. Then, 20 minutes after the alarm sounded, a "perfect gale commenced," Nathan wrote, "and lasted until the next morning." When the calm gave way to heavy winds, there was nothing – or no one – that could stop

Aftermath of the fire, sketched from the Mills House looking north.

what came to be known as The Great Fire of 1861.

Witnesses would later say they were amazed by the speed of the fire. The *Mercury* reporters on the scene would describe a night of chaos unlike anything Charleston had ever seen.

"Before ten o'clock the fire had begun raging in several different points in the lower part of the city. The buildings in the stricken neighborhoods were mostly of wood, old, closely built and surrounded by small out-buildings of an exceedingly inflammable character. As tenement after tenement was first licked by and then enveloped in the fast spreading flames, the panic became awful. The fierce and roaring march of the fire was indeed a horrid scene; but far more heart-rending was the sight of hundreds – we ought, perhaps, to say thousands – of poor and bewildered families, driven suddenly from their homes, destitute of even scanty effects. All the available carts, drays, handcarts and wheel-barrows, were immediately brought into requisition; but these were altogether inadequate to remove even a tithe of the movables beyond the reach of the devouring element."

The nor'easter that descended upon the city stirred a nasty brew of dust and smoke that left most people blind. Those who could see were horrified by "great flaming bits of wood" that were blown nearly a mile southwest of the fire, moving the blaze along even more quickly. The whole city was lit up in a dreadful glare, the paper reported. It was the sight of a fire spreading fast. By 11 p.m., the out-buildings behind Institute

Hall, nearly a half-dozen blocks south of Hasell Street, were aflame.

As the wind pushed the fire into the city's center, it seemed that all of Meeting Street would be lost. Guests at the Mills House ran out into the street, certain the hotel would soon succumb to the flames. As their customers fled, the Mills House staff covered the hotel's walls and roofs with wet blankets. Their quick work ensured that at least one building on the street was saved.

Fanned by the heavy wind and fueled by an endless supply of wooden buildings, the fire grew to monstrous proportions. Confederate troops 14 miles away on Johns Island could see the flames from their camp. Many begged their commanding officers to let them rush to the city, either to check on their families or to help put out the fire. Even Union transport ships, delivering more troops to the lower South Carolina coast, reported seeing the flames six miles out at sea. To those sailors, it looked as if there would be no city left to take.

Every available man in Charleston joined the fight. There were 22 engines on the scene that night, and the firefighters were joined by Confederate military personnel, slaves and free blacks. "One of the most gratifying incidents of the fire of Wednesday night, was the zeal manifested by our slaves, in their efforts, as firemen and laborers," Rhett would later note. But the fire was too large to be contained by twice as many men. The *Mercury* reported that the "Chief and his Assistants, as well as the several companies, exhausted themselves in their efforts to control the flames; the result proved that the elements were too strong for them."

Nothing in the city was safe once the fire began moving. Between Market and Queen streets, every building on the east side of Meeting Street was aflame. By midnight, the Circular Church was burning down. Next door, Institute Hall — where the Democratic Party had fallen apart in the spring of 1860, and where the Ordinance of Secession had been ratified a year earlier — began burning as well. The building that had been dubbed "Secession Hall" would not survive the night.

So many houses and businesses were on fire that workers hardly knew where to start. One team fought to save the East Bay Street home of L.W. Spratt, and might not have succeeded if it hadn't begun to rain – one of the only blessings that night. But the rain was not enough to save the Charleston Hotel or Charleston Theatre as the fire indiscriminately cut a path across the city.

Through it all the streets were filled with thousands of people on their way to becoming homeless. They could do little but watch as nature did what the Yankees only dreamed of doing. The *Mercury* reported that "masters and slaves could be seen working together in removing the household goods and valuables. We noticed one instance particularly, where a white-haired old body servant was giving way to his feelings — sobbing bitterly — at the loss of the family mansion."

This slave noted he had lived in the home his entire life.

Many people were able to save some of their belongings, but few could stop the fires from taking their homes. Some of those who tried, including the firefighters, were injured. And at least one slave woman burned to death when she ran into her master's residence "to save some articles belonging to her mistress." Perhaps the most amazing thing was that more people weren't killed that night.

At 3 a.m. the Circular Church's steeple fell. By then the wind had shifted and it appeared the Charleston Hotel and the Lutheran and Unitarian churches would be safe. But St. Andrew's Hall soon found itself in the path of the blaze. Locals broke into the burning hall and retrieved the full-length portrait of Queen Victoria that had been hanging inside. But no one could save the building.

A year to the month following the state's secession, the two buildings that figured most prominently in the event were destroyed within a few hours. The *Mercury* would later lament, "Those who, but a short year ago, were witnesses of those soul-stirring scenes which ended in Secession, will deeply regret the demolition of the Institute."

This view of the Mills House Hotel comes from years after the fire of 1861, but shows damage inflicted on the building by the flames. Library of Congress photo

Some would no doubt take it as an ominous sign.

At 5:30 on the morning of Dec. 12, the "majestic spire" of the new Cathedral of St. John and St. Finbar fell. This marked the end of the fire, or at least the end of the worst part of it. The flames jumped Broad Street and cut a swath all the way to the river, burning until just after daylight. The last building to fall was W. Izard Bull's mansion at the foot of Tradd Street.

In its wake, much of Charleston had been destroyed.

"In the lower part of the city the fire has done its work in thorough style," Rhett wrote the following day. "Its path is now burned out, and nothing now remains to mark where it has passed, save smouldering piles of cinders and gaunt and smoking walls and chimneys."

It took a week to tally the city's losses.

That Thursday business was "universally suspended" as the community tried to dig itself out of the ashes. Every day the *Mercury* kept a running tab of the losses: "Horlbeck's Alley (from Meeting) to King Street is in ruins," "Church Street, from the corner of Market to Cumberland, is also burned." And later: "The residences on Tradd Street, from Logan to Savage, on either side, with Greenhill, Limehouse and Council streets are, with one or two exceptions, all in ruins."

Charleston was no stranger to fire damage; the city had been plagued with destructive flames throughout its history. In 1740 one blaze claimed 300 houses and in 1788 another 250 were lost in fire. Dozens more were lost in a series of fires throughout the 1830s. Those had been devastating losses, and led to stringent fire codes for private residences, but they paled in comparison to this disaster. Fire Chief Nathan – who eventually lost his initial report of the fire to Confederates – later estimated that the 1861 fire destroyed 1,300 houses and buildings.

For more than a week the *Mercury* devoted one column each day to architectural obituaries of some of the colonial mansions lost in the fire. One of those honored was the Pinckney mansion on East Bay Street, where folks often drank to the memory of George Washington at parties hosted by Charles Cotesworth Pinckney, the legendary politician and South Carolina delegate to the 1787 Constitutional Convention.

The day after the fire Mayor Charles Macbeth issued a proclamation appointing more than a dozen local residents, including former Slave Mart owner Z.B. Oakes, to a relief committee. "The calamitous fire which has spread through our city, upon all who have been within its reach, inflicts loss and suffering. But there are many who, in its ravages, have lost so much, that the aid of all who have been fortunate in escaping its effects, should be, and will be, generally offered for their relief."

By the weekend, "soup houses" were open to feed those left homeless by the fire. The relief committee raised money for the victims, the *Mercury* reporting the names of donors, and the amounts they gave, for several weeks. Soon, a report came in that the Georgia Legislature voted to send $100,000 in aid to Charleston. This was some help, but little could be done. There was no way to replace all that had been lost.

The fire burned 145 acres of the peninsula, a swath that was one mile long and one-seventh of a mile wide. Locals estimated the damage at up to $8 million — nearly half of that in real estate. Charleston spent the rest of the year, and much of the next, cleaning the streets of debris. But it took far longer to repair the city's facade. For the remainder of the war, Charleston lay in ruins, looking as if the city had already lost.

Four days after the fire Susan S. Keith lamented the permanent damage done to the city in a single night of terror and distress. "The city [is] nearly destroyed... It is a doomed City – It was without a doubt the work of our enemies. ... No such fire has ever occurred on the American continent. ... Charleston is no longer a desirable place of residence." Susan Rose Rutledge later wrote to Mary Chesnut, a frequent visitor to the city, that "Charleston looks like a mutilated body! The first impulse would be to turn away and hide your face!"

But there was no way to avoid the fact that this fire had changed Charleston forever.

The year got no better for the city in its final weeks. A week after the fire, Union ships tried once again to take Rockville. Firing from the ships was so heavy that Confederate Col. J.L. Branch of the First Regiment Rifles ordered his men to retreat. The *Mercury* struggled to salvage good news from the incident.

"Fortunately for us, there is a good stretch of solid ground between us," Rhett opined, "and before they go much farther they will have to leave their gunboats behind them, and stand where we can get at them with the bayonet."

But the Union fleet was not merely sneaking up on Charleston from behind. Yankee ships were beginning to congregate outside the harbor in greater numbers, threatening to cut off the city's link to the rest of the world. The Union's blockade plans were taking shape and the Confederate troops could do nothing to stop this. In fact, the military was soon forced to inflict even more damage on the city. On Dec. 20, the *Mercury* ran the headline, "Charleston Lighthouse Blown Up and Destroyed."

The lighthouse, "situated on Morris Island, and which for many years has guided the mariner into our harbor, was blown up on Wednesday night, by order of the military authorities. Nothing save a heap of ruins now marks the spot where it stood."

Charleston would end its first full year of independence from the U.S. government much less optimistic than it had been in the heady days following secession. The city in shambles, the enemy closing in by land and by sea, there was little reason to heed Rhett's Christmas wish in the *Mercury* to "not give way too far to these depressing influences."

And then, on New Year's Eve, another fire scared the city. It was merely a pile of boards that had gone up — nothing the firemen couldn't handle. Still, the small blaze was attacked fiercely by locals, a scene more heartening that any calls for patriotism from Rhett.

Charleston was down, but the fight had not gone out of her.

The Stone Fleet

CHAPTER 9

TROUBLED WATERS

The ships arrived on a Monday night. Between eight and 10 of them, mostly sailing barks or brigs, quickly fell in line with the other federal ships attempting to block all traffic into and out of the harbor. This was an ominous sight, a line of towering masts on the horizon that stood between Charleston and the rest of the world.

By the following morning — Jan. 21, 1862 — Charleston residents still picking through the ruins of the December fire took time to spread the word that the Yankees were stepping up their attempts to cut off the city's supply lines. These ships were not simple blockaders, however; many did not appear to even be warships. The *Mercury* reported that "some of them seem to be old craft, and do not resemble armed vessels in any respect."

That led most people to assume the North had sent in another stone fleet. In December, the United States Navy sunk 16 ships in the channels leading into Charleston Harbor. They were mostly old whalers – junk that the Union bought at reduced rates. The ships were filled with New England granite and then scuttled to serve as barricades. The wrecks would either stop traffic or tear the keel out of any ship that didn't yield. Locals dubbed these ships "the stone fleet."

Now, it seemed that first round was only the beginning, that soon there would be even more shipwrecks cluttering the channel.

All of this went along with the Union's Anaconda Plan. The strategy was to blockade every southern port from the Mississippi River up the East Coast, depriving

Southern coastal cities of all supplies — much as Maj. Robert Anderson's men had been forced to do at Fort Sumter. The plan was not executed very well; there weren't enough ships to guard the Mississippi, and efforts on the East Coast produced mixed results. The U.S. Navy had a particularly tough time with Charleston. There were simply too many routes into the harbor.

In December the sloop-of-war *Pocahontas* tried to stop a Confederate steamer from sailing out of Stono Inlet south of Folly Island. The *Pocahontas* fired a couple of shots at the boat, but the steamer quickly slipped by and made it safely out to sea. Meanwhile, two batteries on Cole's Island opened fire on the *Pocahontas*, sending it scurrying toward the horizon.

The *Mercury* kept a running tally of these blockaders; there were rarely more than five ships or fewer than three – not enough to do an effective job. Blockade runners and privateers were still finding their way into port, selling their goods at greatly inflated prices to reflect the risk they had taken. But the New Year brought a new resolve from the North to clog up the most important Southern ports, Charleston undoubtedly one of them. Still, the morning after this new batch of ships arrived, Robert Barnwell Rhett Jr. discounted speculation that these vessels were part of another stone fleet.

"It is, we think, more likely that these vessels are all from the Port Royal fleet, and that they have been ordered hither merely to keep up a more efficient blockade, for they are strung in single file across the harbor entrance," Rhett wrote in the *Mercury*.

But Rhett's theory didn't hold for long. The next day lookouts for the city spotted the crews of this new batch of blockaders stripping the ships of all rigging and spars. One of the recent arrivals had already been scuttled between Beach Channel and Rattlesnake Shoal, just a few miles off Sullivan's Island.

"This no longer left any room for doubt that this was really another detachment of the famous Stone fleet, by which the wicked City of Charleston is to be 'hermetically sealed,'" the *Mercury* reported.

Rhett quickly amended his earlier analysis and predicted that most of the remaining ships would be sunk during the night to avoid observation. A nor'easter soon blew up, giving the Yankee sailors fits and slowing their work considerably, a fact that Rhett took great joy in reporting. But the fact remained that Charleston Harbor was being bottled up. The only good news was that, as a result of the storm, the city's wells were finally filling up again.

Loaded with New England granite, the old ships were sunk to block access to the harbor.

Most of the second stone fleet sunk during the last week of January. The movements off the coast held the attention of Charleston residents for more than a week, the *Mercury* providing regular updates. Most days, Rhett noted, the weather was too rough for any work at sea and the Union fleet could do little more than hold its position off the bar. But everyone knew it was only a matter of time until the Yankees carried out their plans – winter weather never lingered for long in Charleston.

Union soldiers took advantage of a break in the storms on Sunday, Jan. 26, to send most of the old ships to the Atlantic floor. By the *Mercury*'s tally, the blockade fleet sunk 10 wrecks, which brought the total number of channel obstructions to 26. Slowly, the U.S. Navy was proceeding with its plans to ensure that Charleston was closed for business. The proof washed up within days. In early February refuse from this second stone fleet — spars and blocks, mainly — were found floating in the harbor. Local sailors claimed that winter storms were breaking up the wrecks, and began collecting the trash and hauling it ashore.

"Many of the smaller specimens are being distributed over the city, and will, in time, be among the curiosities of the Lincoln War," the *Mercury* reported. "Others, that are more valuable, are being sold by the wreckers."

While Charleston residents were reduced to selling junk dumped in their water by

The U.S. Navy took great pains to stop blockade runners from leaving or entering Charleston. Many of them ended up beached on local sea islands, including the *Ruby*, a British-built blockade runner that was intercepted by the federal squadron in 1863.

the Union Navy, Northern newspapers were crowing about the progress made by the blockade. On Feb. 4 the *Mercury* reprinted an article from the New York *Tribune* that called Maffitt's Channel just off Sullivan's Island "one of the rat holes to Charleston, and a more important one than we were led to suppose." The Navy planned to soon sink several ships from the stone fleet in Maffitt's, the paper reported, which would cut off one of the blockade runners' favorite routes.

"This will relieve us of a troublesome channel to guard," the *Tribune* noted.

Charleston remained consumed by news of the blockade for much of the winter. The *Tribune* reported the Navy ships would remain outside of Charleston for the foreseeable future, and no evidence existed to contradict that claim. The entire war seemed to have shifted to the sea. Soon rumors surfaced that Union ships were advancing on Savannah and parts of the North Carolina coast. Some speculated that Bull's Bay between Charleston and Georgetown had been targeted.

By the middle of February it became clear that was another story with a bit of truth to it.

On Feb. 14, the U.S. Navy captured the schooner *Theodore Stoney* as it crossed the bay about 20 miles north of Charleston. A single Union vessel had stopped the *Stoney* early that morning, its officers demanding the captain's papers and any firearms he might have onboard. After the crew produced a single gun – the mate's revolver – the Yankees commandeered the ship. According to Capt. Roberts, the *Stoney*'s master, the Lincolnites meant to sail the boat to Port Royal. But these sailors knew nothing of the notoriously shallow bay and quickly ran the boat aground.

The frustrated Union sailors offered Roberts money to pilot the ship out of the bay, and even claimed Admiral DuPont might give him his ship back once they reached open water. But the captain knew better than to believe that. He refused, and the angry Yankees burned the *Stoney* to the waterline. For reasons unclear to Roberts, he and his son were released soon afterward. Crews on the schooners *Elizabeth* and *Wando*, as well as the sloop *Edisto*, witnessed the burning of the *Stoney* and panicked. Fearing their ships would be next, the crews sank all three ships and escaped to the mainland.

The incident highlighted Charleston's — and the Confederacy's — greatest weakness, a flaw in the Southern defenses that had become all too apparent with the fall of Port Royal. A month earlier Rhett had outlined the problem in the *Mercury* when he posed the question: "Shall We Build a Navy?"

"It has ceased to be a matter either of doubt, or concealment, that the ease with which the enemy has mastered our bays and inlets, is due less to the peculiar topography of our sea islands, than to our utter want of strength on the water," Rhett had astutely opined. "We have been taught, by bitter experience, the impossibility of providing adequate land defences for the numerous bays and inlets of our coast. For the security of our seaboard, a navy is absolutely essential, and any attempt to avoid the outlay, necessary to maintain an extensive armed marine, would indeed be poor economy."

For nearly a year, most of the South had concentrated on the ground war and ignored perhaps its most glaring weakness. The North recognized this and exploited it, first at Hatteras and then at Port Royal. Even with its early flaws, the Anaconda Plan was a stroke of military genius. But this escalation of blockading efforts and the growing number of attacks on Southern ships would force the Confederacy to come around to Rhett's way of thinking.

The events off Virginia cinched it.

On Saturday, March 8, the South launched the CSS *Virginia* in an assault on the blockading squadron near Hampton Roads. The former *Merrimack* was a simple steam frigate, but it looked nothing like its former self. Salvaged by Southerners, the ship had been refit as a ram with a deck made of iron sheathing nearly four inches thick. When the *Virginia* sailed out of the Elizabeth River, it was the debut of an entirely new kind of warship.

On that day the South controlled the water. The *Virginia* sank the sloop-of-war *Cumberland* and inflicted heavy damage on the *Congress*, a U.S. Navy frigate that proved no match for the iron ship's guns. The Confederate ship chased a third vessel, the *Minnesota*, until it ran aground. The *Virginia* returned to port for repairs that afternoon, but came back the next day to finish the job. And there, the former *Merrimack* met the USS *Monitor*, standing between it and the crippled *Minnesota*.

The Union Navy's own ironclad had been designed by John Ericsson, a Swedish engineer. It was built partly in response to intelligence the Navy received about the Confederates' refit of the *Merrimack*. The *Monitor* was a curious sight: its hull sat low in the water, protected by iron, and featured a rotating gun turret – a development almost unheard of at the time. It would become the model for an entire fleet of warships. The U.S. Navy would call them Monitor-class ironclads, and Charleston residents would come to know them well.

For three hours that day the two warships fired at one another, neither able to do the other much harm. The *Virginia* finally damaged the *Monitor*'s pilothouse, but could not get around the ship to finish off the *Minnesota*. The battle was a draw, although the *Monitor* was able to prevent the *Virginia* from breaking the federal blockade. But the battle held even more significance: The era of the ironclad had arrived.

Over the next week the Charleston *Mercury* devoted several pages to the battle, heralding it as the South's first naval victory of the war. The appearance of the *Monitor* only solidified Rhett's opinion that the South had to build its own Navy. Within a week the newspaper would suggest that Charleston follow the lead of Virginia and refit the *Mackinaw* and *John Ravenel* with gun decks and roofs made of railroad iron.

"Nothing ought to be left undone to break up the blockade," Rhett suggested, "and patriotic men, instead of buying up vessels in port for speculative purposes, ought rather to afford every facility in their power to make the most of the material at hand for war purposes."

It was a sly condemnation of war profiteering disguised as patriotism. And it was quickly answered, but not exactly as Rhett intended.

Inspired by similar campaigns in New Orleans and Mobile, Susan Lining Gelzer wrote to the editor of the *Charleston Courier* suggesting the city build its own gunboat. The 30-year-old woman claimed several of her friends would be willing to assist in the fund-raising and asked that the newspaper publish notice of the new fund. It could be a ladies' campaign, and she opened the account by sending along $5.

"If every true woman in our beloved State would contribute the same amount we would soon be enabled to give an order for more than one gunboat," Gelzer wrote.

The *Courier's* editor, Richard Yeadon, took Gelzer's idea and promoted it ceaselessly in the newspaper. It was, to his mind, just the sort of thing to lift Charleston's spirits. "Our women have brave hearts and liberal hands," he wrote. "They are fully awake to the dangers of the crisis and fully alive to the impulses and duties of patriotism; and if occasion requires, they will nobly emulate the conduct of their Revolutionary mothers."

To the chagrin of Rhett, the *Courier* had co-opted his idea for a Southern navy and was gaining great publicity around the city in the process. The first $2,000 raised for the boat went directly to the *Courier* offices. Rhett could only insert himself in the campaign by promising to forward any donations sent to the *Mercury*. It was not an ideal situation, but soon even Rhett was collecting donations, cheered on by his call "build *Merrimacks* for every Southern harbor, and build them at once."

The fundraiser quickly took on a life of its own and offered Charleston residents a chance to get involved with the war effort. The newspaper even came up with a contest so that readers could vote on names for Charleston's own ironclad gunboat, which was already under construction. Readers who wrote in to express support for the idea soon agreed on a name.

They decided it would only be fitting to christen Charleston's first ironclad the *Palmetto State*.

Robert Smalls

CHAPTER 10

THE STRAW HAT RUSE

The ship steamed by Fort Sumter two hours before daybreak, blowing its whistle to the guards on night watch as it passed. It moved neither fast nor slow and followed the channel naturally, skirting the shore of Sullivan's Island. The corporal of the guard glanced at it just briefly before calling out to Capt. Fleming, officer of the day. It was only the *Planter* passing through, he reported.

It was a vessel the fort's officers knew well. The 147-foot, shallow-draft steamer – a cotton boat, the locals called her – had been chartered by the Confederate government and moved from the Pee Dee River to Charleston, where it served as a dispatch boat for Gen. Roswell S. Ripley, the Confederate Army's district commander. The boat ran letters to the troops on Morris Island and carried responses back to the general. Its chief value was its slight draft, which allowed it to easily navigate shallow Lowcountry tidal waters.

Even at that early hour, 4:15 a.m., there was no reason for suspicion. The *Planter* often made the run to Morris Island at odd times; there was always something going on. That morning, May 12, 1862, the corporal of the guard simply reported its appearance, as he was supposed to do, and went about his business. He would later recall that someone on the *Planter's* deck even waved at him. He assumed it was the boat's captain, C.J. Relyea.

After all, he recognized the captain's straw hat.

The fading light of a nearly full moon allowed the bored sentinels to watch as the *Planter* chugged into the channel that morning. All boats to Morris Island followed the same course: they sailed out far beyond the fort and then suddenly turned south. For a while the ship followed that well-worn route perfectly. But when it reached the point where it was supposed to turn, the *Planter* revved its engines and sped out to sea on a course to intercept the U.S. Navy's blockading fleet.

It would be hours before the confused men at Fort Sumter realized that they had been duped by a half-dozen runaway slaves.

The loss of one of the Confederacy's precious ships could not have come at a worse time for morale in Charleston. Locals still were struggling to recover from the fire that had decimated much of the old city in December and news from the front had been dismal for more than a month. The battle at Shiloh, which the *Mercury* initially reported as a Southern victory, had quickly turned to disaster in the Tennessee countryside.

Gen. P.G.T. Beauregard had led a surprise attack against Union Gen. Ulysses S. Grant, meaning to drive the Yankees away from the Tennessee River and into the swamps. For the first day of fighting the Confederates appeared to have the upper hand, but on April 7 Union reinforcements arrived and turned the tide. Ultimately, more than 3,000 men were killed in the battle, another 16,000 wounded. To that point, it was one of the bloodiest battles in American history. And although the casualties were divided nearly evenly between the two forces, it was the Southerners who were forced to retreat.

Then the Yankees struck closer to Charleston. On April 10 Union forces attacked Fort Pulaski in Georgia, which guarded the river leading into Savannah. By the next day, the U.S. Army – using rifled cannons – penetrated the brick fort's walls, forcing the Confederates to surrender and effectively cutting off Charleston's sister city from the sea. It was a crushing defeat for the Southerners. The raw destructive force of the Yankees' new rifled cannons did not bode well for Fort Sumter, many locals noted.

Before the month was out, the Confederates suffered a third humiliating loss. After a week of fighting, Union forces took New Orleans in late April. The largest city in the Confederacy had fallen, and with it the spirits of most Southerners. Robert Barnwell Rhett Jr. was so distraught that he could scarcely provide any reassurance to Charleston. In a front-page editorial, the *Mercury* editor asked, "Is Charleston to be Saved?"

"Our people and the State authorities must make up their minds either to throw the ordnance of our Forts into the sea, and blow them up, evacuating Charleston to the enemy, or they must see that our harbor is obstructed and Fort Sumter secured from Parrott guns on Morris Island," Rhett opined. "The time has fully come to face this alternative and the sooner we get a conclusion the better. Groakers are a useless class. We repeat that, in our opinion, Charleston can probably be saved by prompt and untiring energy."

The rant was a not very subtle attempt to stir patriotism, which had flagged noticeably since the initial excitement of the war. After the Confederacy's successful start – winning at Sumter, at Manassas – a series of setbacks had caused enthusiasm and enrollment in the military to wane. Even before the setbacks of April, the number of volunteers joining the Confederate Army dwindled so much that the state was forced to enact a conscription law.

The law called for all men between the ages of 18 and 45 to enroll, but included a provision that gave wealthy citizens a convenient escape clause. Anyone who could afford to do so was allowed to hire someone to serve in their stead, assuming that person was not already a member of the militia. The *Mercury* endorsed the conscription and astutely noted that the campaign should have come sooner, when it would have been far easier to attract new recruits. Now, given a string of victories by Union forces, a draft seemed the only way to keep pace.

Most men signed up without complaint, arriving at Market Hall to gather their supplies, their weapons and their orders. Although the upstairs room served as offices for the city market, it had been used for dances on occasion. It was a large, airy room with three ornate gas chandeliers and floor-to-ceiling windows – as fine a meeting room, in some ways, as Society Hall. Many of the men who passed through its oversize doors would remember Market Hall fondly and return to it often in later years.

Soon after the conscription began there was some unexpected grousing among the working class when the newspaper published a list of people exempted from the law. It included members of Congress, the state Legislature, ferry men, mailmen, boat pilots, professors and newspaper journalists among them. Between those exemptions and the loophole for the rich, the *Mercury*'s claim that conscription was more likely to "insure equal justice to all the arms-bearing citizens of the State" seemed like a cruel joke.

At the same time, state officials did nothing to improve their standing when they considered an outright ban on the distillation and sale of whiskey. They claimed the corn was needed to feed the troops, a plausible explanation, and said the shortage of grain had made it difficult to feed the Army's horses. But there was more to it than that. The move had as much to do with morals and morale – troubling times sent a greater number of people seeking refuge in a bottle. And that did nothing to help the Confederacy's war efforts.

"Drunkenness is the great and growing sin of these troublesome times, and the instant abatement of the nuisance is absolutely necessary to save our army from demoralization and our people from becoming a nation of sots," Rhett opined in the *Mercury*.

By the end of February, Mayor Charles Macbeth ordered police to close all bars in Charleston. The saloons would remain closed until further notice – but not without a fight. The bar owners took the city to court, a legal question that would remain unsettled for months. In the meantime, the ladies of the city hosted a Grand Fair to raise money for their gunboat and enliven spirits, so to speak. Over the course of several nights in early May, hundreds of residents made their way to Hibernian Hall for raffles and ring-cakes and parties that stretched into the night. Gov. Francis Pickens even made an appearance, greeting locals and sampling exotic drink concoctions. But there was no liquor, a point that even the *Mercury* lamented.

"But the lack of juleps and Roman punches does not prevent the Fair from being a most delightful entertainment," the paper noted.

As festive as the occasion was, local woes could not be banished with a simple – and sober – party. Less than a week after the fair ended, city officials put Charleston under martial law. The *Mercury* attempted to portray the move as beneficial, predicting locals would conform to military regulations "cheerfully." But there was more to it than that, as Rhett had to concede. There were simply too many soldiers in town, and there had been too many problems for the local police force to handle alone. One of the most common complaints was that some of these troops had been harassing the women of Charleston.

"It has repeatedly happened, within the last few days, that ladies have been mildly accosted and insulted by soldiers, in the public thoroughfares," the paper reported. "In some instances, outrages of the most flagrant character have been committed, with perfect impunity, by men wearing the honorable uniform of Southern volunteers. We

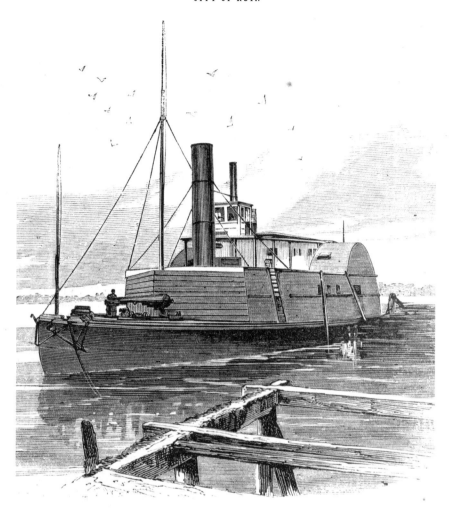

The *Planter*

do not know who the offenders are; but we do know that, in the City of Charleston, such acts cannot and will not be allowed to continue."

That same day, as Charleston was coming to terms with the realities of living in a war zone, a plot was hatched by one industrious slave.

Robert Smalls had very little in common with most South Carolina slaves. He had lived on his own in Charleston for nearly a decade, most days moving through the city like a freedman. His wife was a former slave and his children were free. The uncommon level of liberty that Smalls enjoyed in 1862 Charleston was a nod to his negotiating skills, his intelligence and, perhaps, his background.

The 23-year-old mulatto had been born in 1839 in a slave cabin behind John McKee's Beaufort home, where his mother worked as a house servant. He was Lydia Smalls' only child, and the identity of his father was a mystery. Some believed he was the son of Moses Goldsmith, a wealthy Jewish merchant from Charleston. Others thought McKee himself was Smalls' father, which may have explained his relative freedom.

Smalls was sent to Charleston when he was 12, the idea being that he could make McKee more money in the city. For six years Smalls worked as a waiter, a stevedore and eventually a sailor, sending his pay – save for $1 – to his owner. By the time he was 18 he had negotiated a new deal with McKee, one that allowed him to keep all but $15 of his wages. Smalls would put the money to good use.

In 1856, when Smalls was only 17, he married Hannah Jones – a hotel maid and slave who was nearly twice his age. They soon had a daughter, named for Smalls' mother, and within a few years he saved enough money to buy his wife and daughter from their owner. He was planning to purchase his own freedom when his son, Robert Jr., was born in 1861.

That year Smalls took work as a deckhand on the *Planter*, Gen. Ripley's dispatch boat, and soon he was its pilot. Even though he still sent $15 of his salary to McKee, it was not a bad job – Smalls realized there were certainly worse occupations for men of his station in life. As the pilot aboard Ripley's boat, Smalls overheard the secrets of the Confederacy and learned the routines of Charleston's waterfront. He soon found a use for all that knowledge.

Smalls reported to Charles J. Relyea, the *Planter*'s captain, a short and stocky man with a number of affectations. Relyea was well known on the waterfront for his wide-brimmed straw hat, which he wore whenever he was on the boat. It was his trademark. One afternoon when the *Planter* was docked at the Southern Wharf at the east end of The Battery, one of the slaves who worked on the boat found Relyea's straw hat in the cabin and decided to have a little fun. The man carried it outside, snuck up behind Smalls and put the hat on his head – just joking around.

The horseplay continued for a few minutes until someone strolling along the dock stopped and noted that, from a distance, he had mistaken Smalls for Captain Relyea.

After all, they were roughly the same height and had the same build. But the hat had cinched it. Smalls would not forget that offhand remark – it gave him an idea. All he needed was an opportunity, and it came within weeks.

On the night of May 11, Relyea and his crew left the *Planter* unattended. There were rules about that sort of thing – someone from the crew was always supposed to be aboard the general's boat. But on this evening Relyea and his men snuck away. Although it was a breach of protocol, the crew had to make an early run to Morris Island the next morning. Perhaps they only wanted to steal an early evening at home.

Sometime after midnight, when it was quiet on the waterfront, Smalls and seven other men – all slaves – casually made their way toward the boat, greeting the sentries as they passed. At the time no one thought anything about it. These men worked indirectly for Gen. Ripley and few guards would risk his ire by questioning them.

Smalls and the other men loitered on deck for hours, pretending to keep busy for the benefit of passersby. They did not want to make any move until the deadest part of the night when there would be fewer men on duty should anyone try and stop them. About 3 a.m., Smalls told one of the men to fire up the *Planter*'s engine. They waited a while longer, just to see if the noise attracted any attention. But no one came.

Less than a half-hour later, the men cast off and the *Planter* set sail.

The sentries on the docks never suspected anything was amiss. It didn't even seem odd when the *Planter* steamed upriver and rendezvoused with a Confederate ship called the *Etowah*. Any guard who noticed the ship's movements simply assumed Captain Relyea and his entire crew were aboard the boat. It was a mistake destined to be repeated several times that night.

Smalls' wife and children – along with the families of the other *Planter* slaves – were hiding aboard the *Etowah*, where they were smuggled aboard with help from two black stewards. All night they waited for the signal to emerge from their hiding places. Once the *Planter* pulled alongside, it took only a few minutes to transfer their families and one of the Etowah stewards onboard. And then Smalls turned the ship toward the harbor's mouth.

The most crucial moment of the operation came at 4:15 a.m. as the *Planter* drifted into range of Fort Sumter. Smalls knew the fort had more than enough firepower to easily sink the boat if soldiers there suspected anything. To make sure that did not happen, Smalls had planned a show for the guards at Sumter. It was time to test the observation of the man he'd met on the docks weeks earlier.

As the boat drifted within sight of the fort, Smalls donned Captain Relyea's straw hat and, as he later told it, "stood so that the sentinel could not see my color." He ordered the correct whistle signal – two long blows, then a short one – and then he waved to the men at Sumter. He kept up the charade for several tense minutes as the *Planter* chugged alongside the fort and out into the channel.

Smalls maintained a normal speed as the ship steamed out to sea. He had to take care not to tip off the sentries while the *Planter* was within easy range of Sumter's guns. When he reached the mark to make the expected turn to Morris Island, Smalls sped up quickly and made for the blockade.

It would be hours before anyone at Sumter realized what had happened.

As Smalls approached the blockading squadron, he quickly ordered his men to lower the *Planter's* Confederate banner. In its place, his men hoisted a white bed sheet to signal the boat's surrender. Smalls would later tell a crowd of admirers in New York that, as he pulled alongside one of the blockade ships, the Union sailors erupted in cheers.

The U.S. Navy sent the hijacked *Planter* to Port Royal and gave Smalls a job. Eventually they would name him the boat's captain, making him the first black commander of a U.S. ship. By the end of his first month as a free man, the United States Congress awarded Smalls and his crew half the estimated value of the *Planter* and its cargo in cash, giving them more wealth than most citizens could claim. A decade later, during Reconstruction, Smalls would join Congress as a representative from South Carolina.

The loss of the *Planter* was a considerable blow. The Confederacy did not have a surplus of ships, especially those with the unique features of a shallow-draft cotton boat. But as it turned out, the cost for the South was even higher. The *Planter* was loaded the night before with cannons that were due to be shipped to Morris Island for defense of the city. Now the Yankees had them.

In Charleston the fallout continued for weeks. Relyea, his first mate and engineer were eventually court-martialed for leaving the *Planter* untended, although their sentences were rescinded when it was argued that no one had ever explained to Relyea the rules about leaving the ship. That technicality did not prevent Rhett from chastising the men in the *Mercury*, arguing that, "The result of this negligence may be only the loss of the guns and of the boat ... but things of this kind are sometimes of incalculable injury."

Rhett may have been referring to Charleston's perpetually declining morale but the warning was more prescient than anyone realized at the time. Smalls not only gave the Yankees the *Planter* and four new guns; he supplied them with valuable intelligence he overheard while working on the dispatch boat. He told U.S. Navy officials that the shorthanded Confederates were abandoning Cole's Island and Battery Island, two spits of land that guarded the mouth of the Stono River.

That bit of intelligence would allow Navy ships to sail undetected into the river and land on the far side of James Island. And the Union commanders quickly decided the west side of James Island would make a fine place from which to attack the troublesome city of Charleston.

The Battle of Secessionville

CHAPTER 11

SECESSIONVILLE

T he ship was running quiet and fast, hugging the shore of Dewees Island, trying to reach Charleston Harbor before first light. The crew sailed from Nassau
with hopes of slipping past the blockade gunboats and sneaking into the city, where
they could sell their cargo of medicines and general supplies. It was a great risk, but
one that could reap ample reward – if they survived.

But like so many others, the *Nellie* would not make it.

The blockade had cut off Charleston's trade lines and supplies in the city were running perilously low. Any ship that made it into port was assured a handsome profit
by selling whatever it had at black-market rates. It mattered little what these ships
hauled – Charleston needed almost everything. On a weekly basis the newspapers
reported the price locals were paying for these supplies, usually without comment:
zinc nails, 17 cents per pound; Imperial tea, $6 per pound; carbonate of ammonia,
$1.75 per pound. It was just another cost of war.

Captain Moore was wise to avoid the southern route, the most popular course into
the city. Instead, he sailed the *Nellie* north out of the Bahamas, passing Charleston
while far out at sea, then back-tracking along the coast north of the city. Fewer ships
tended to congregate at the northern end of the blockade. Still, as the first strains
of light broke the horizon on Sunday, May 25, 1862, the bow watch on one Navy
schooner quickly spotted the *Nellie*.

Once again, Charleston residents would awake to the sound of cannon fire.

The *Nellie* had few options. Moore's course certainly was the best way to make it
into Charleston, but it had one serious flaw: It left his ship trapped between the sea

islands and a line of warships. Once the *Nellie* was spotted, the crew's sole option was to outrun the blockaders to the harbor entrance, where Forts Sumter and Moultrie would no doubt fire on any Yankee ship that came within range. It was Moore's only hope – his unarmed steamship was no match for the Union Navy. He ordered his crew to speed up.

Of course, the blockading fleet anticipated Moore's move – the U.S. Navy had some experience in this field. No sooner than the *Nellie* cranked up its engine several ships blocked its path. Then the Union boats opened fire in unison, a barrage that unnerved Moore and his crew. If the *Nellie* continued on its course, it was clear the Yankees would not hesitate to sink it. Moore had only one choice if he wanted to survive. He ran the ship aground on the beach at Long Island.

For the rest of the day crews worked to unload the *Nellie*'s cargo, both to save the merchandise and lighten the ship's load. Confederate batteries on the island provided a covering fire to keep the blockaders away, but they were of little use against the tide. That night heavy seas pushed the *Nellie* farther ashore. The ship was beached and by Monday the Yankees were using its hull for target practice. Another blockade runner out of business.

The fate of the *Nellie* was just another unwanted reminder of Charleston's precarious situation. The blockade bottled up the harbor, there were reports that Union gunboats were in Georgetown and Union troops out of Port Royal were spotted at a plantation on the Combahee River. On May 29 Confederates engaged some of those troops at Pocotaligo. It was quickly becoming clear that the city was surrounded. In an uncharacteristic bit of understatement, Robert Barnwell Rhett Jr. lamented in the *Mercury* that "The Yankees hereabouts are becoming bolder every day."

The showdown was inevitable.

Union troops had been making their way north from Port Royal since the winter, methodically moving from one island to the next. The ultimate destination — and prize — was Charleston, of course, but there seemed to be no hurry in their movements until May. Just weeks after the former slave Robert Smalls told U.S. Navy officials of the weaknesses in the South's Stono River defenses, the Yankees decided to test that intelligence.

On June 2 Union gunboats sailed into the river between Folly and Kiawah islands and began firing shells in the vicinity of the Tower Battery outside Secessionville, a James Island neighborhood with a name that pre-dated the state's independence. The following day, Union troops went ashore and the fighting began almost immediately. Throughout June 3 Charleston residents heard the echo of gunfire as the two forces clashed below Secessionville, a minor battle that took place under continuous rain that covered the island in heavy mist. Eventually the Southerners pushed the Yankees back to the river, and the Irish Volunteers captured 20 Union soldiers near "Mr. Legare's house."

Most people realized that this was only a prelude to a much larger and important battle. The next day, the *Mercury* declared "Our Day of Trial at Hand." The paper reported rumors that the Burnside Fleet was massing offshore, but predicted that "unless they have a number of Monitors," they would pay dearly for trying to run the Confederate gauntlet.

"Our people are calm, and prepared for desperate resistance," the *Mercury* reported. "We have everything at stake in the struggle, and little to hope in case of failure."

Neither Confederate nor state officials were under any illusions about what was at stake. If the Union took James Island, it would become extremely difficult for the South to hold Charleston. And the loss of the city would be devastating. Gen. Robert E. Lee himself had opined that, "The loss of Charleston would cut us off entirely from communications with the rest of the world and close the only channel through which we can expect to get supplies from abroad, now almost our only dependence."

South Carolina officials understood this as well, and Gov. Francis Pickens and his executive council responded to the build-up of federal forces with a resolution that declared, "Charleston should be defended at any cost of life or property, and that in their deliberate judgment they would prefer a repulse of the enemy with the entire city in ruins to an evacuation or surrender on any terms whatever."

These mandates were clear, but the Confederates could not help but feel that, despite the urgency of the situation, they were getting little support. Every day brought new orders that called local troops to some other far-away battlefield. Real concerns surfaced that, should an invasion actually come, there would not be enough troops left in Charleston to fend it off.

After the capture of Union soldiers at Legare's house, little activity ensued on the islands until the weekend, when Col. Dunnovant encountered a "force of Yankee ma-

Bayonette charge of Union troops in the Battle of Secessionville.

rauders" on Johns Island. The Confederates attacked, driving the Union troops across Haulover bridge, even taking the bags of supplies dropped by the retreating Yanks. Then, on Saturday night, some local troops captured a Union picket on James Island.

By Sunday afternoon Northern soldiers infiltrated the island's interior deep enough to attack Confederate pickets on the road between Fort Johnson and Fort Pemberton. There the Confederates again repelled the Union soldiers and killed a number of the attackers. But the night was not a total success for the South. At least four privates on picket duty were taken prisoner.

It could have been much worse. More than 6,000 Union troops — two divisions — had landed on James Island and were encamped near Grimball Plantation. They outnumbered Confederate troops on the island by roughly 3-to-1 but the impressive resistance of the Southerners persuaded the North to proceed cautiously. Maj. Gen. David Hunter told Brig. Gen. Henry Benham not to attack without further orders.

The Confederates, by contrast, were in no position to hesitate. Union prisoners

disclosed that 16 regiments were on the island with more expected to arrive every day. The battle for Charleston was at hand – and the Southerners had to strike first. On June 10 the Confederate forts on James Island began shelling the Yankee troops, as well as their gunboats, in the Stono River. The attack was announced by cannon fire that rattled downtown Charleston for most of the day.

At 3:30 that afternoon, Brig. Gen. Johnson Hagood's regiment attacked the Union troops at Grimball Plantation. It was an ordeal just to get in position. Hagood's men trudged through nearly a mile of pluff mud and swamp, but once they emerged from the marsh the troops showed no sign of fatigue. In short order the regiment managed to push a superior number of Union forces backward about 300 yards, almost to the banks of the river. The Southerners thought they had the battle won, but then the Union gunboats joined the fight, firing in concert with Yankee batteries on the island.

"The concentrated fire of the enemy's batteries, gunboat and musketry were so murderous that our little handful of men, unsupported, were compelled to retire, after having suffered a heavy loss," the *Mercury* reported.

Later, Confederate military officials estimated Hagood's regiment suffered about 50 casualties that afternoon, most coming as the heavy shelling forced their retreat. The only good news for Charleston, according to the *Mercury*, was that, "The enemy's loss is believed to be heavier than our own." For the moment the two sides appeared to be at a standstill, merely swapping blows.

For the next week the two sides fought intermittently across James Island. The North and the South were engaged in a dangerous dance, engaging violently for brief moments before retreating to opposing corners. These skirmishes rarely amounted to much or lasted very long and were followed by long periods of nervous silence which the *Mercury* reported with headlines such as "All Quiet on James Island." It was clear to everyone this was merely prelude to the real battle.

On Sunday, June 15, Confederate troops discovered a small battery of Yankee Parrott guns at the edge of the woods, a spot the 47th Georgia defended only days before. From that position, the Union opened fire on one of Col. Thomas G. Lamar's batteries, a barrage of shells that eventually resulted in one casualty: Pvt. John H. Andrews. Then, sometime between 9 and 10 p.m., locals spotted a bright glare in the direction of Dill's Bluff. It was not another firefight, but simply precaution. The Confederates burned Dill's house, presumably to keep it out of enemy hands. Before the night ended the Southern troops took further precautions, which turned out to be a wise move.

The Yankees were antsy. Brig. Gen. Henry N. Benham felt he had waited long enough for orders to attack, and it seemed they might never come. Feeling he had a good number of troops and the tactical advantage, he made the decision to send his troops into the interior of James Island during the early hours of June 16. There, he meant to end this battle once and for all. But he would soon learn the Confederates anticipated his every move.

The Southern troops spent much of the night preparing for a pending Union assault. About 500 troops at the Tower Battery worked into the early morning at Secessionville, building additional batteries to support and defend the M-shaped fort. Lamar pushed his men until 3 a.m., when they finally collapsed, fatigued, in the fields around the fort. They were so tired that for once the men were allowed to sleep without their hands on their rifles. It turned out to be a poor time to relax the rule.

An exhausted Lamar was asleep on the fort's parapet around 4:30 a.m. when one of his pickets woke him. The man reported that his patrol had been overrun by a huge force of Yankees headed their way. It was not much of an advance warning; the picket estimated the troops were only 50 yards away. It didn't matter that the Union soldiers were actually somewhat farther out; there was little time to react. The battle was at hand.

Two divisions were marching toward Tower Battery, each numbering more than 3,000 men. They set out for Secessionville at 2 a.m., while the Confederates were still working. Many of the men carried unloaded guns and were under orders to remain silent and attack the fort with bayonets. As soon as they reached the field in front of the fort, the Confederate gunners at Tower Battery – awakened by one of Lamar's junior officers – spotted them.

It was an awesome sight: a horde of soldiers running toward the fort, bayonets fixed. Lamar, shaking off his fatigue, estimated they were about 400 yards away. As soon as he saw the sheer number of men in blue, he sent one of his officers to Fort Johnson, five miles away. Get reinforcements, he told the soldier. Quickly.

Lamar ran to one of the bigger guns in the fort, intent on firing the first shot. He reached an 8-inch Columbiad that was already loaded and pulled the lanyard. Just before it fired, however, he heard the report of a 24-pounder that had beaten him to the punch. The Battle of Secessionville had begun.

It all happened so quickly. Lamar's men began "pouring grape and canister against the rapidly approaching enemy," the *Mercury* would report the next day. "At each discharge, great gaps were visible in the Yankee ranks, but still they came on, without firing a single volley."

At first Lamar assumed the Union soldiers were simply out of ammunition. It was much later before he learned that most of the soldiers – many of them men of the 8th Michigan – meant to sneak up and attack the fort's personnel with bayonets. But they lost the element of surprise. As the 8th Michigan reached the fort, the 1st S.C. Artillery's gun split the regiment in two.

For a while the Union troops kept coming, both sides taking casualties. When the 79th New York was late in arriving to back-up the 8th Michigan, the fire became "too severe for their nerves" and they fled in disorder. But not before several Southerners, including South Carolina native Julius A. Shuler of the 1st S.C. Artillery, fell. He would become one of the many soldiers to die in defense of Charleston.

The Union kept coming. Shortly after the first wave of troops fell apart, the men in blue re-grouped and charged again – this time reinforced by infantry and artillery. This attack brought "heavy volleys" against the Lamar batteries but soon the Southerners had the advantage once again, mowing down the advancing men.

The Union soldiers fared only slightly better on their third attempt to charge the fort. Some of the Northern troops crossed the ditch near the battery, but when they came out of it on the near side of the fort, the *Mercury* later reported, they paid for their efforts with their lives. Neither side was spared on this morning. Just before the third wave began, Col. Lamar was hit by a minié ball in his neck. As he struggled to stop the bleeding and maintain consciousness, he turned command over to Lt. Col. Gaillard.

Eventually the two sides fell into hand-to-hand combat, a bloody exercise in mutual destruction. The 8th Michigan lost a third of its men in the fighting, the reward for leading the assault. The brutal scene and the determination of Union troops, particularly the 8th, earned the Yankees a measure of respect from their adversaries – and even from locals.

"Our men all bear witness to the obstinate bravery of the enemy on this occasion," Rhett wrote in the *Mercury*.

As the Confederates repelled the ground attack at the fort's walls, federal gunboats in the Stono fired on Tower Battery and federal flanking columns formed in a last effort to take Secessionville. The Union forces fired across the marshland to the right of the fort, but any success they might have had was lost when the 4th Louisiana Battalion, which had been camped two miles away, arrived and took the advantage. But by then it was almost over.

Hours of gunshot and cannon fire left James Island awash in smoke. The Tower Battery's commander was down, although he would survive, and the field in front of the fort was littered with bodies. No one would ever agree on the number of men who died there, but it was clear that in five hours of fighting several hundred men were killed. And then, just after 9 a.m., the battlefield fell silent.

The Yankees were retreating.

A collection of little more than 2,000 Confederate troops had fought off more than

6,000 Union soldiers, one of the more amazing statistics of the war. Although Secessionville would never be considered a major battle of the Civil War, it certainly would have qualified had it gone the other way. Gen. Lee's prediction was never forgotten: If the Union had taken James Island, leading to the fall of Charleston, the rest of the war might have unfolded differently. Certainly it would have been a shorter conflict.

Instead the battle turned into a disaster for the Union. Benham was ordered to Hilton Head Island, where he was arrested three days after the events at Secessionville. He was charged with attacking without orders, and promptly blamed it on another officer. Ultimately Benham was relieved of his command. Maj. Gen. David Hunter replaced Benham with Brig. Gen. Horatio Wright. Hunter's instructions were even clearer this time, according to *The Seige of Charleston*.

"You will not attempt to advance towards Charleston or Fort Johnson till largely reinforced and until you receive express orders from these headquarters," Hunter said.

Charleston would bask in the glow of victory for weeks. Southern troops had not received such adoration from the city since the war began at Fort Sumter. Not long after the battle, a Charleston girl asked one of the Secessionville veterans, who had been wounded in the fighting, why the Confederates didn't retreat when faced with such an overpowering show of force.

"Where could we have gone other than the bottom of the Ashley River," the soldier said, "for had we crossed over to the city, you would have beaten us out of it with your broomsticks."

This was exactly the right response, and the city enjoyed the sort of celebratory mood it needed after months of worry over a pending Yankee invasion. The local troops rose to the challenge, and the legend endured in Charleston for more than a century. But it was the larger message of Secessionville that most excited Robert Barnwell Rhett Jr.

"It seems that the Yankees no longer rest under the hallucination that Charleston, like Nashville and New Orleans, is to fall into their hands without a desperate struggle," the editor wrote in the June 25 edition of the *Mercury*.

For the first time in months, the newspaper was able to report some good news.

The *Chicora* and *Palmetto State* in Charleston Harbor.

CHAPTER 12

THE PALMETTO STATE

It was unlike anything that had ever sailed into Charleston Harbor. The ship was 150 feet long with a low, flat deck that barely cleared the waterline. The middle was dominated by a steep, sloping iron-clad deckhouse with a single smokestack. Peeking out of this floating fortress were the barrels of four considerable guns – two smooth-bore, two rifled. In profile it looked like a floating butter dish, albeit one armed to the teeth.

On Saturday morning, Oct. 11, 1862, the residents of Charleston crowded the docks at Marsh Wharf, just a few blocks north of the Market, for a glimpse of this curious new addition to the harbor fleet. Not even a sudden rain, which drenched the crowd before abruptly dissipating, could dampen the spirits of the hundreds of people who had turned out to witness the baptism of Charleston's first, and locally built, ironclad gunboat.

The *Palmetto State* was ready for battle.

Seven months after the first clash of ironclads at Hampton Roads, the city finally had its own lethal gunboat. This was thanks in part to the numerous ladies of the city, many of whom were crowded on the docks. For months, the "Ladies' Gunboat" association raised money for the ship's construction, ultimately contributing nearly $30,000 to the cause. These women sold baked goods and needlepoint, hocked swords and silverware off their own shelves. One woman raffled off a set of French china.

On this day, they would be honored for their commitment to the war effort. Several were given prominent seats atop the ship's deckhouse for the ceremony. From that

The *Palmetto State*

perch they watched the arrival of honored guests, including Col. Richard Yeadon –
editor of the Charleston *Daily Courier* – and D.N. Ingraham, who later served as the
ship's captain. Yeadon in particular was invaluable in promoting the fundraising
efforts and received a hearty cheer of appreciation from the crowd.

That applause would pale, however, in comparison to the raucous celebration that
broke out at the appearance of Gen. Pierre Gustave Toutant Beauregard, recently
returned to the city. As he took his seat among the ladies, the "assembled throng"
welcomed him with "hearty and long continued cheers," the *Mercury* later reported.

Yeadon delivered the ceremony's main address, speaking loud enough to be heard
easily over the distant thunder of a looming storm. He declared the ship's name "redo-
lent of victory," recalling the Revolutionary War battle in which the troops on Sullivan's Island repelled the British fleet with a fort made of palmetto logs. The *Palmetto
State*, Yeadon predicted, would "prove herself not unworthy of that glorious name."

When the speeches ended, Sue Gelzer – the young woman who suggested the
idea of the Ladies' Gunboat campaign and contributed the first $5 to the fund – was
escorted to the *Palmetto State's* low foredeck. Without speaking a word she smashed
a bottle of "choice old wine" on its bow. The editor would do the speaking for her.

"With all solemnity and reverence," Yeadon said, "and invoking on thee the blessing of Almighty God, noble boat, *Palmetto State*, I baptize thee, in the name of the patriotic ladies of South Carolina. Amen."

The celebration continued into the afternoon with a luncheon at the workshop on Marsh Wharf, where some work on the boat had been completed. For hours, spectators filed by for a closer look at the strange ship. Just as the official ceremony ended, the remaining crowd saw a ship steam by that was nearly the *Palmetto State*'s twin. The *Chicora*, the *Mercury* noted, would likely be finished and ready for a similar send-off within 90 days. It appeared the city would soon have a fleet able to take on the Union blockade.

The ceremony ended with three cheers for the gunboat and three more for its unfinished sister ship.

The *Palmetto State*'s christening could not have come at a better time. After the victory at Secessionville, Charleston struggled through an unsettling summer. As the war dragged into its second year, enthusiasm for the conflict seemed to have waned slightly. It did not help that locals felt increasingly isolated, cut off from the rest of the South. These factors took their toll, and throughout the hottest months a series of bizarre events dominated the local news.

Local authorities discovered a counterfeiting ring operating out of the city. A member of the Charleston Light Dragoons was accidentally shot by friendly fire. Then, on July 16, the military raided a small store on Anson Street, seizing "two dray loads of what appeared to be whisky and other spirits." A woman in the store tried to stop the guards from searching the premises and when they attempted to apprehend her, she crashed through the front window and took off running. Severely cut by the broken glass, the bleeding woman ran to the Market, procured a pistol and returned to protect her property.

"Notwithstanding the violence of the woman," the *Mercury* reported, "the guard exercised the greatest moderation towards her."

The next day a gun exploded at Fort Moultrie during a routine inspection, killing Lt. Col. Thomas W. Wagner. Few locals were more committed to the war effort than Wagner. The former state lawmaker and rice planter had raised an entire company of men after the state seceded and took part in the battle of Fort Sumter. The *Mercury* reported that the senseless occasion of Wagner's death "spread gloom" over the entire city.

"Few men in our midst could have been as illy spared," the *Mercury* noted.

Throughout the summer it seemed most of the local Confederates' woes were self-inflicted. Wagner's death followed another unfortunate accident at Green Pond. During an arms inspection one soldier got his carbine tangled in his reins, causing it to discharge. The ball hit Pvt. T.W. Clagett in the head, passing all the way through and killing him instantly. August ended with the execution of Cpl. George H. Burger of Company E, 1st Regiment, S.C. Artillery, who had been charged with desertion. After his court-martial, Burger was shot on the beach at Sullivan's Island, "some little distance beyond the Moultrie House."

Two war-related deaths in Virginia also contributed to the moribund tone of the local news that summer. The son of *Courier* editor Richard Yeadon died in the Battle of Chickahominy at Hanover County, Va. Then 22-year-old Robert Woodward Rhett – son of *Mercury* editor Robert Barnwell Rhett Jr. – was killed in a charge near Richmond. The editors restrained themselves and made little mention of the deaths, but Rhett in particular seemed to step up his criticism of the Confederacy. He blamed the politicians for not devoting enough resources to protecting Charleston. Those who knew him likely thought that some of Rhett's pain was showing through in these increasingly combative editorials.

The city's mood improved somewhat in early September when the *Mercury* reported the "important rumor" that Gen. Beauregard was believed to be en route to Charleston, which would become his headquarters for defense of the coast. Most still regarded Beauregard as one of the South's greatest generals and credited him with the glorious victory at Sumter. The newspaper soon reported that the hero of "Manassas and Shiloh" arrived in town on Saturday, Sept. 13, and checked into the Mills House. By the month's end, Beauregard would take the Meeting Street home of Otis Mills as his residence and headquarters.

"We are sure that his presence will stimulate the minds of our troops and people with his own unconquerable spirit, and that his knowledge, judgment and energy will speedily supply whatever may be lacking to render Charleston safe against the enemy's attacks," Rhett opined in the *Mercury*. "The eventful campaigns of the last two years have afforded abundant evidence of the tact and success of General Beauregard in the management of large armies of volunteers."

No one — not even the newspaper editors — realized that Beauregard was not at all pleased to be back in Charleston.

The general had been unceremoniously relieved of his command in the West and was less than happy about it. The official reason for this reprimand was that Beauregard retreated from a critical rail line in Corinth, Miss., the previous May. He did so only because his men were greatly outnumbered by advancing Union troops and sick from drinking contaminated water, which left them in no condition to fight. But that mattered little to Confederate President Jefferson Davis, who did not particularly like Beauregard anyway. When the general took medical leave without permission soon after the events at Corinth, he was ordered back to Charleston. His friends tried to intervene with Davis, but to no avail.

Ultimately Beauregard was a good soldier; he did what he was told. He spent the fall strengthening Charleston defenses and was often seen around the harbor making inspections at Forts Sumter and Moultrie. This time he did not bother with public relations tours; he had no stomach for it and probably realized the locals didn't either.

The Rebel Rams engaging the blockading fleet off Charleston.

Charleston residents spent the fall much as they passed their summer, distracted by incidents that had little to do with battles. On Nov. 15, G.V. Anker discovered a runaway slave named Charles loitering near his Coming Street house. The *Mercury* later reported that Charles, "belonging to Mr. J.K. Brown," had been on the run for two years and was "known to be a desperate fellow." When the police cornered Charles and he realized that he could not escape, the slave drew a knife and slit his own throat. He died almost instantly.

Two weeks later, Phillis Stuart, a free black woman, was arrested and charged with "sending a mulatto child to a school for white children." The mayor sentenced Stuart to 30 days solitary confinement. "We understand that there are some other cases of this character," the *Mercury* reported, "which will soon be looked after."

As winter approached, a series of skirmishes suggested the lull in local fighting was drawing to an end. Confederate troops repulsed Yankee forces trying to make inroads south of Charleston at Pocotaligo. And a small boat from the blockading fleet snuck close to Sullivan's Island one night to take soundings, prompting the Beauregard Battery to welcome "the venturesome boat with a shot ... causing the occupants to skedaddle in hot haste." Then Union gunboats shelled James Island in retaliation. On New Year's Day the *Mercury* hoped for a glorious 1863 to wash away "this winter of our discontent."

"The darkest days of our trial, we trust, are passed. The Old Year is gone, with its long months of carnage. The New Year can scarcely unfold so red a record of suffering, disaster, and dear-bought triumphs."

This was yet another prediction that Robert Barnwell Rhett Jr. would soon be forced to amend.

The first weeks of the New Year brought little relief. It seemed that the South's predicament grew worse with each passing day. A shortage of corn threatened the South, and then two ships were captured trying to leave the harbor before the British steamer *Calypso* managed to avoid cannon fire and reached the city with "valuable cargo." The good news, for Southerners, was all happening elsewhere. The dreaded Union ironclad, the *Monitor*, was lost in a storm while under tow off the Outer Banks. Soon after that, a Yankee gunboat was captured off the Florida coast.

Although it was not a particularly good month for the Union Navy, the blockade outside Charleston Harbor seemed just as effective as ever. For every ship that reached port several others were captured. Locals began to notice the Confederates' lack of progress in breaking the blockade. On Wednesday, Jan. 28, the newspaper printed a letter from a local sailor that succinctly summed up the frustrations of the entire city.

"Why is it that, with gunboats at this port, well armed, manned and officered, and 'spoiling for a fight,' we do not clear the blockade?"

Since the baptism of the *Palmetto State*, its sister ship, the *Chicora*, had joined the harbor fleet but neither ironclad had done much – as the letter signed only "A Mariner" pointed out. In truth, the Confederates knew there were inherent problems with their newest weapons. The gunboats were cramped, slow and so heavily weighted down by their iron skins that they drew 12 feet. That meant they could barely cross the bar to get outside the harbor. If any enemy ships got within the range of either ironclad, it would be too late to save Charleston.

Ever sensitive to public perception, Beauregard must have seen the letter in the *Mercury*. He recognized that the lack of action from the two ships threatened the city's tenuous morale and knew the boats would not improve with age. He quickly urged Ingraham to take the *Palmetto State* outside the harbor for military maneuvers. If he could sink an enemy ship, it would be a bonus.

On Friday night, Jan. 30, the *Palmetto State* and the *Chicora* slipped away from the docks around 9. They were followed by three boats that would serve as tenders, including the *Etiwan*. The ships crept along, not only because of their limitations but also because Ingraham did not want to reach the bar until after the moon had set. If any blockader saw the ships, no escape would be possible. In a light breeze and calm seas, the two ironclads managed to get across the bar without incident.

And there, outside the harbor at last, they waited.

Just after 4 a.m., a lookout aboard the *Palmetto State* spotted the silhouette of a Yankee ship dead ahead. The gunboat slowly gathered steam and laid in a course for the USS *Mercedita*. Fifty yards out, the *Palmetto State* helmsman cut the engines and allowed accumulated momentum to propel them toward the Union ship.

The *Mercedita* had been part of the blockade outside Charleston since September, and in that period had seen scarcely any action. For that reason, the sailors on the wooden steamer were unprepared for what was coming. The captain was half-dressed, asleep in his cabin and had only a small crew on deck watch. One of those men eventually spotted the *Palmetto State,* but did not recognize that its course was intentional, or even that it was an enemy ship.

"Back her, or you'll run into us," the sailor called out.

Of course, that was Ingraham's plan.

The *Palmetto State* rammed bow-first into the *Mercedita's* port quarter, ripping a hole in the ship's keel. As the concussion of the impact subsided, the Southerners fired their forward gun into the blockade ship, bursting its boiler and immediately crippling its engine. By the time the *Palmetto State* began to back away, the *Mercedita* captain – still not dressed – signaled his surrender.

As one engagement ended, another began. The *Chicora* had snuck up on the USS *Keystone State,* a side-wheel steamer that had been stationed off Charleston for a year. The crew of the blockader spotted the *Chicora* and fired. The Southerners returned fire three times before hearing the *Keystone State*'s fire bell. Still the Yankee sailors kept shooting back.

The *Chicora*'s crew called out to the *Keystone State,* ordering the ship's surrender. At first they got no response and didn't understand why. One of the Confederates' shots ripped into the *Keystone State*'s steam drum, an explosion that killed 20 men. But the remaining crew would not give up. As the *Chicora* crew awaited a reply from the damaged ship, another U.S. Navy side-wheel steamship, the *Quaker City,* pulled up behind their gunboat and began firing.

As those two ships traded blows, the *Keystone State* managed to sail beyond the reach of the Southern guns. The *Mercedita* – not damaged as badly as the *Palmetto State* crew believed – followed in its wake. Some other Navy ships came in, firing from a distance that was safely out of range of the ironclads. The two sides traded shots until nearly sunrise, when the fight dissipated. Eventually the *Palmetto State* and the *Chicora* steamed for shore. The tides conspired against the tired crews, however, and they were forced to wait until the afternoon for enough water to carry them across the bar and into the harbor.

While the two ironclads swung at anchor during that long day, their bored crews surveyed the horizon, a seascape devoid of detail – and devoid of the Union Navy. Although the *Palmetto State* and the *Chicora* had not taken a single ship, they had at least briefly dispersed the blockade. Gen. Beauregard would be pleased by the outcome of the engagement, although he harbored no illusions that the blockade was over.

The ships would be back, he knew, but he had renewed faith that Charleston was ready for the coming fight.

Bombardment of Fort Sumter and adjacent forts by the Union fleet.

CHAPTER 13

INVASION IMMINENT

The gunboats sailed into the Stono a little farther every day, quite literally testing the waters. They would creep through the inlet and make the first few bends in the river, sometimes shooting at scattered Confederate troops on James Island before slipping back out to sea. This game began in the fall of 1862 and continued into the winter, the Yankees growing bolder each week. The Union Navy was trying to extend the limits of its reach into South Carolina and in the process had become just enough of an annoyance to prevent the Confederates from fortifying the riverbanks.

The boldest and most troublesome of these ships was a converted river steamer called the *Isaac P. Smith*. More often than not, this was the boat that made these irritating incursions. The sight of the ship infuriated the Southerners because it was so brazen. The captain, Lt. F.S. Conover, allowed his bored crew to pass the time by taking target practice at houses along the river — or any person who wandered into view. Once the sailors even landed a boat at an abandoned Johns Island plantation and drew a picture of a man on a carriage house. During several subsequent trips, the sailors amused themselves by shooting at their crude artwork.

When Gen. Beauregard got wind of this behavior, he decided to make an example of the *Isaac P. Smith*.

It was an elaborate plan, perhaps more complex than the situation demanded. Beauregard quietly ordered some men to move several heavy guns to James Island and hide them near the riverbank on Thomas Grimball's plantation. At the same time, other guns were moved to Johns Island. Soldiers later claimed they hid some of the cannons in bales of hay. Two of the guns were stowed inside the carriage house that was defaced with the Yankee artwork.

By Thursday, Jan. 29, 1863, the trap was set. But for once the *Isaac P. Smith* failed to show. The Confederates were not dissuaded; they knew it would be back, and they would wait as long as it took. That turned out to be only one more day.

They spotted the ship on Friday afternoon just as it passed Grimball's plantation. It was following its normal course, sailing so close to the shore that the Southerners could make out the faces of the lookouts on each of the boat's three masts. But the Union lookouts did not see the Confederates until it was too late. Capt. John H. Gary watched the ship creeping along less than 100 yards offshore, waiting for his moment. When the *Isaac P. Smith* was in the perfect spot, flank exposed to the shore, he ordered his men to open fire.

The first shot ripped through the ship's timbers, an audible crash that the Confederates could hear from shore. The troops could see the men scurrying about on deck and heard one officer cry out, "Great God! What is this?" The *Isaac P. Smith* had been taken completely by surprise.

The ship began its retreat immediately but the Union sailors regained their composure enough that they were returning fire even as they tried to escape. For a moment it seemed as if this ambush might turn into a real fight. The *Isaac P. Smith* took out one of Gary's guns with a single shot and killed one man as the sailors continued to hurl fire at the riverbank. But soon the troops on Johns Island joined in, getting off three good shots in a row – one of which took out the gunboat's engine.

Within seconds, the *Isaac P. Smith* belched white steam from its smokestack. The ship then dropped its anchor and Conover offered his unconditional surrender. In the brief fight, 19 Union sailors were killed and six others were wounded. When the Confederates took the ship they found a good bit of money onboard, which they delivered to Gen. Ripley. Revenge was, for the South, most profitable that day. And it was also something of an historic engagement.

It was one of the first times in history that a warship had surrendered to field batteries.

Beauregard was worried.

Every intelligence report that landed on his desk in the winter of 1863 suggested the Union Navy was planning a major assault on Charleston. In early February, Capt. Charles Haskell captured two officers from the Union gunboat *Flambeau* on Bull's Island. A day later the British steam frigate *Cadmus* arrived off the bar carrying news that an expedition of formidable character was being assembled and "the enemy is now nearly ready for an attack." Finally, on Feb. 17, the *Mercury* published a report out of Savannah which claimed Yankee troops from Hilton Head Island were overheard discussing plans to invade Charleston the following Sunday.

Despite the successes of the *Palmetto State* and the *Chicora*, and the capture of the *Isaac P. Smith*, Beauregard did not think the city's naval defenses were all that improved – at least not enough to fend off a full-scale invasion. Even Robert Barnwell Rhett Jr. realized this. In a series of front-page editorials about "The Expected Attack," the *Mercury* editor said that Charleston had serious work before it. "The fight in the harbor between our batteries and the iron-clad gunboats is going to be an experiment, concerning which we and the world have no experience from the past. Although we are hopeful of the result, we should prepare to fight the city itself in defence."

The day after the overheard Yankee gossip made the paper, Beauregard had Rhett

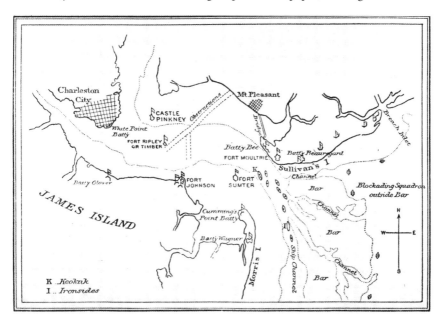

The path of Union gunboats in the attack on Fort Sumter.

The Union Fleet prepares for battle.

publish a letter in the *Mercury* that warned of a possible attack and stressed the general's hope that "all persons unable to take an active part in the struggle" would get out of town. Beauregard's note left the entire city on edge. When a Yankee gunboat approached Sullivan's Island on Saturday, locals feared the assault was under way. But troops on the island quickly spotted a white flag flying from the *Flambeau*. The boat was simply delivering mail for the captured crew of the *Isaac P. Smith*.

For weeks after that incident, Charleston was quiet – but the dread of impending attack was never far from anyone's mind. The next scare came on March 12 when heavy and rapid artillery fire erupted before daybreak across the harbor. For two hours the shooting continued unabated and the reason remained a mystery in the city. Many believed that, finally, the Yankees were coming.

As it turned out, the first shots were simply a test of battery signals in the event of an attack. But someone didn't get the memo and soon batteries around the harbor joined the shelling. Two shells from Fort Sumter caused a scare on Sullivan's Island. One shot whizzed over Battery Bee and another went through a house with the owners inside. Luckily, the house was the only casualty of the day.

As the winter thawed, Beauregard was increasingly distracted by arcane points

of law. Several Southern attorneys maintained that when an enemy fleet blockaded a harbor, they must give ample notice of their intent. These attorneys convinced the general that if the fleet was dispersed for even a brief amount of time, the legal process has to begin again. And many people believed that the late January attack by the *Palmetto State* and the *Chicora* had, however briefly, broken the blockade.

Beauregard tried to use the quaint law to clear the channel, but the U.S. Navy refused to budge or even concede the blockade had been disrupted. On March 7 the *Mercury* published a letter sent to the newspaper by officers of the blockading fleet that said, "No vessels were sunk and none set on fire" during the attack by Charleston's ironclads. They claimed the *Mercedita* and the *Keystone State* were slightly damaged, but that was all. The two sides may have been wary of engaging in a naval battle but they were more than willing to snipe at each other in the press.

The war of words did not divert Beauregard's attention so much that he failed to notice an increase in the number of blockade ships off the coast. More ships arrived each week, but still some blockade runners managed to elude the federal fleet. On March 17, the *Ruby* arrived from Nassau and sold its cargo for a substantial profit. The next day, the British steamship *Calypso* outran Union gunboats and dodged

The bombardment viewed from Morris Island.

heavy shelling to reach the wharf in Charleston. By the time a third ship tried the next day, the blockade was better prepared.

Around 1 a.m. on Thursday, March 19, the British steamer *Georgiana* reached the South Carolina coast carrying medicine, dry goods and six pieces of field artillery for Charleston. Off Dewees Island, the ship sailed past a schooner and a steamer without being spotted. But that luck would not hold. A third blockade ship spied the *Georgiana* and opened fire with deadly efficiency. One shell passed through the ship and another exploded under the stern, taking out the rudder. To escape capture, the *Georgiana*'s captain ran his ship aground at Long Island. The crew quickly flooded it to keep the Union Navy from taking the vessel and its cargo. Charleston, desperate for supplies, lost a much-needed cache of goods.

On March 30 the *Mercury* reported "unwanted activity" by the enemy off the coast. In the last week pickets had spotted a fleet of 21 ships in the North Edisto River. Among the boats were at least four turreted ironclads. Over the weekend, "intelligence reports" noted that a gunboat and three transport ships had approached Cole's Island at the mouth of the Stono and landed some 200 troops there. The Yankees were finally ready to attack. But the Union fleet's heart wasn't in it.

Rear Adm. Samuel F. DuPont spent the winter preparing to attack the city but he still didn't think the fleet was ready. He learned of Beauregard's improvement to harbor defenses, and DuPont had considerable respect for the general's military prowess. There were rumors that the entrance to Charleston Harbor was lined with mines and it frustrated DuPont that he could not confirm this bit of intelligence. If that weren't bad enough, the admiral was not particularly happy with his ironclads.

After putting the gunboats through a series of tests, DuPont concluded that the *Patapsco*, *Passaic* and *Nahant* were slow and quick to break down — similar to the problems that afflicted Charleston's own ironclads. DuPont decided these ships were no match for the forts protecting Charleston. But officials in Washington insisted that he press on with his plans and DuPont was not a man to ignore orders, even if he had his misgivings.

By the time the *Mercury* declared "The Hour At Hand" on Tuesday, April 7, Beauregard had ordered all women and children to leave the city. The command went largely ignored, despite the apparent proof of a pending invasion. The newspaper noted that day that nine ironclads — "eight turreted Monitors and the *Ironsides*" — as well as 30 wooden ships had appeared off the bar the day before.

"At all events, their movements were such as to induce the anticipation that the thunders of conflict will be heard before our next issue shall meet the eyes of our readers," Rhett wrote.

Confederate military leaders were expecting an amphibious assault. The *Mercury* reported that the Union would again send ground troops onto James Island. But this would be primarily a naval battle. And even though it was one-dimensional, it was an impressive assault. At 2:30 that afternoon, the ironclad *Weehawken* began advancing on Fort Sumter, the Union fleet spread out behind it in attack formation.

Charleston reverberated under the "dull detonation" of the first shot of the battle at 3 p.m., when Fort Moultrie trained a heavy gun on the lead ship. When the shot had no effect, the Confederates realized the ships were not in range yet and would not waste ammunition on errant shots. The Southern guns stood down, waiting for the enemy to draw in closer. As they advanced, the U.S. Navy ironclads returned fire, each shot leaving white puffs of smoke hovering over their turrets. At first, their shells did little damage.

At 3:10 Fort Sumter joined the fray, opening her guns on the fleet as batteries on Sullivan's and Morris islands provided additional firepower. The Confederates had 76 guns trained on the fleet and while the Navy ships kept coming, they were soon overwhelmed by the barrage. The *Passaic* fired four shots in quick succession but

Advance of the ironclads

the ironclad took two devastating blows in return – one of which hit the lower part of the ironclad's gun turret, disabling it. The Yankee gunboat would eventually take 35 hits in 35 minutes.

The *New Ironsides,* the most intimidating ship in the blockading fleet, ultimately played little role in the assault. The ship's deep draft limited its course in the shallow water off the coast and it eventually collided with two other ships in the fleet. At one point the *New Ironsides* was floating just above one of the Confederate mines as DuPont had feared. Engineers on shore tried to detonate the mine, but it malfunctioned and would not fire. It was one of the few breaks the Union Navy got that day.

By 4:30 Charleston Harbor was blanketed in smoke, the battle "fierce and general" as the long line of Union ironclads peppered shots at Moultrie and some of the small batteries. One shot took out the fort's flagstaff and killed a private named Lusby. Soon the gunboats would turn all their efforts on the eastern face of Fort Sumter. The fort was hit repeatedly, but the damage was minimal – some straw bedding caught fire and one shot sent a shower of bricks onto Sgt. Faulkner and the men of Company B. A few soldiers were injured in the melee and another shot tore the fort's Confederate flag.

The Union fleet would not get off so lightly. Aboard the *Weehawken*, Capt. John Rodgers felt his ship shudder from one shot and thought it was an underwater mine. Worried that he might sink, Rodgers ordered a retreat. Behind him, the fleet soon fell apart. Many of the other ships were struggling with similar damage. The *Passaic* was dead in the water; if it was going to survive, it would have to be towed. In all, the Confederates had scored more than 500 hits on the fleet.

Aboard the *New Ironsides*, DuPont felt helpless. The ship had taken an estimated

93 hits and through the smoke the admiral could not signal the other boats. But he knew the battle was lost. He ordered the *New Ironsides* to begin steaming south, firing a few parting shots at Sumter as it went. Soon the ironclads followed DuPont's lead and broke off just before 5:30.

The ironclad *Keokuk* would become the battle's largest casualty. As the *New Ironsides* came alongside the boat, Capt. A.C. Rhind told DuPont his gunboat had taken heavy shelling and was undoubtedly sinking. Eventually the crew had no choice but to abandon ship just off Morris Island. The *Keokuk* sank the next morning. Equipment and furniture from the ironclad washed up on the beach at Morris Island over the next week. Confederates collected some of the debris and ultimately decided to sneak out for a closer look. The Southerners stripped the *Keokuk* of its 11-inch gun, which was mounted at Fort Sumter.

This was the final irony of the battle. Union Brig. Gen. Quincy A. Gillmore later noted that Fort Sumter had "defied the assault of the most powerful and gallant fleet the world ever saw." And the only thing that came of it was a new gun for the Confederate fort.

As the Union fleet limped away to the safe confines of Port Royal, the troops at Fort Sumter held a dress parade and fired guns in salute. Since Secessionville, the Charleston troops had had little to celebrate. Now they had not only repelled the Yankee invasion, they had managed to escape relatively unscathed. It appeared the city could relax.

But as it turned out, the Union Navy's attack was only the opening salvo in the coming siege.

Col. Robert Gould Shaw, commander of the 54th Massachusetts Colored Volunteers Infantry, was killed early in the assault on Battery Wagner.

CHAPTER 14

MORRIS ISLAND

Something about Folly didn't look quite right.

As the night faded to a dull gray morning on July 10, 1863, the island was an indiscernible mass of shapes across the inlet. Still, the Confederate troops guarding the southern tip of Morris Island thought something about it looked different. They stared at the dark mass for several minutes until the dawn came and they were able to make out what they were seeing. On Thursday the northern end of Folly Island was a dense mass of trees and brush. But all that foliage had been cleared away in the night and in its place now stood a Union battery of nearly four-dozen guns.

The Southerners recognized this just before those guns opened fire.

Later, Union officials would boast that the attack on Morris Island was a complete surprise, but that was not the case. For months Charleston residents had known that U.S. troops were gathering on Folly. Military leaders knew they had been on Cole's Island at least since April and two nights earlier, Charles Haskell's scouting party ran across federal barges near Lighthouse Inlet and heard the sound of wood being chopped onshore. The Yankees were up to something.

Minor skirmishes had broken out of late when small bands of Union troops tried to infiltrate James Island, and earlier the Northern troops had fired on Morris Island. Just that morning, the July 10 edition of the *Mercury* reported that an estimated 8,000 Union troops had amassed on Folly, backed up by seven ironclads and 43 other boats. Locals had hoped this build-up was merely for show, and Beauregard had kept most of his troops on James Island, knowing it was the more strategic point for any army that wanted to invade Charleston. But when the Morris Island sentries saw those guns, they realized it was an assault.

The shooting began just after 5 a.m. The Confederates on the southern end of Morris Island were hopelessly outgunned but returned fire for three hours, the sound of their incessant shooting echoing across the harbor and through the streets of Charleston. Around 8 a.m. barges carrying hundreds of Union soldiers landed at Oyster Point, near the island's southernmost tip. Once the soldiers had filed off the barges, the boats immediately cast off and went back for reinforcements. It was a full-scale invasion.

On the beach at Morris Island, the Union troops flanked the Confederate batteries, driving back their infantry support. Capt. John C. Mitchell of the 1st Regiment, S.C. Artillery later reported that he and his men were nearly cut off from the main body of Confederate forces by the sheer number of Union soldiers storming onto the island.

As the Union troops advanced on the southern battery, Mitchell's men stood at their guns, firing and fighting as best they could. But they never had a chance. Ironclads off the beach aided the Union ground troops and shelled the battery while the men in blue trudged north. Soon, the Confederates were overwhelmed.

There were just too many Yankees.

Outnumbered, the Confederates were forced north toward the safety of Battery Wagner. They retreated into the dunes, following the infantry support that had already ceded the lower part of the island. By 9 a.m. Union forces had chased the fleeing Southerners so far up the island that they were within shooting range of Wagner. In little more than four hours, a Union force of 2,000 men had taken two-thirds of Morris Island. They had killed nearly 300 Southerners and injured another 700. By contrast, the North had lost only 12 men and fewer than 100 had been injured. But the Yankees were not finished.

They wanted Battery Wagner.

It had been a bad month for the South.

A week before the Union attack on Morris Island the Confederates lost two major battles on back-to-back days – defeats that would have fatal repercussions. On July 1, Confederate Gen. Robert E. Lee led the Army of Northern Virginia and more than 70,000 troops against Union Maj. Gen. George Gordon Meade in the Pennsylvania countryside. This was Lee's second push into the North and this time he planned to march as far as Philadelphia, a move that he hoped might subdue the Union's appetite for war.

Outside the little town of Gettysburg, the Army of Northern Virginia ran into the more than 100,000 U.S. troops under Meade's command. For three days the two sides clashed in what became one of the most famous battles in history. It was also the bloodiest of the Civil War. Between July 1 and 3, nearly 5,000 Southern troops were killed and 18,000 were injured, captured or missing. The Union, by contrast, lost more than 3,000 men with 14,000 wounded. The battle, which historians would later call the turning point of the war, doomed Lee's push into the North.

A day later, the siege at Vicksburg ended after nearly seven weeks. Union Maj. Gen. Ulysses S. Grant and the Army of the Tennessee had surrounded Confederate Lt. Gen. John C. Pemberton's forces and held them in place for weeks. Pemberton's troops suffered heavy casualties in the initial battle and were running dangerously low on provisions. With no reinforcements coming, Pemberton surrendered on July 4 – a symbolic day for the Yankees, perhaps. Within a week the Union controlled the entire Mississippi River.

At first it seemed that Morris Island would become Charleston's own Gettysburg. The invasion of the island was only the first move in a larger campaign to capture the city. The goal of the July 10 attack had been to move troops into a position from which to attack Battery Wagner on the north end of the island. As Robert Barnwell Rhett Jr. explained in the *Mercury* on July 13, Wagner was the key to the city. This was not Charleston's Gettysburg; it was more akin to the Siege of Vicksburg.

"The fall of Fort Wagner ends in the fall of Charleston," the editor wrote. "Fort Sumter, like Fort Wagner, will then be assailable by land and sea, and the fate of Fort Pulaski will be that of Sumter. ... It appears to be useless to attempt to disguise from ourselves our situation. By whose fault we got into it, it is vain now to enquire. The Yankees having got possession of the southern half of Morris Island, there is but one way to save the city of Charleston, and that is the speedy and unflinching use of the bayonet."

It was a simple plan. The Union wanted to take Battery Wagner to use the fort's advantageous position to attack Sumter. If the Yankees could take out Fort Sumter, Charleston would then become relatively easy pickings. On paper it seemed almost elementary. But Union forces would find several obstacles to their battle plan. Taking the southern half of Morris Island had been easy; taking Wagner would require even more troops — and a lot of luck.

Battery Wagner was named for the late Lt. Col. Thomas M. Wagner, a local patriot who had died in an accident the previous summer. It was a massive earthwork that stretched across the narrow end of Morris Island about a half-mile from its northern tip. The fort itself had 14 guns, one of which was a 10-inch Columbiad that fired a 128-pound shell. More than 1,700 Confederate troops were stationed in and around the fort. The battery was protected from ground assault by a ditch that was 10 feet wide and held 5 feet of water. On its banks, Southern troops had planted mines and mounted stakes made of palmetto. It was a most formidable moat.

The Union would not wait long to make its first attempt to take Wagner. At daybreak on Saturday, July 11, 200 men from the 7th Connecticut sneaked through the dunes, bayonets fixed. They were trying to get as close to the battery as possible before alerting the Southerners to their presence. But when they were about 500 yards out the Confederate pickets spotted them and opened fire.

Instead of retreating under fire, the men of the 7th Connecticut let out a yell and rushed the fort, advancing far enough to clear the treacherous moat. But it took them far too long. They were soon pinned under heavy rifle and cannon fire. This time it was the Southern barrage that was too much for the Northern troops, and the Union forces had to retreat — but not before the 7th Connecticut lost more than half its men. That day there were more than 300 U.S. casualties, many of whom were left lying in front of the earthworks. By contrast, the South had lost only 12 men. In addition, the Confederates captured more than 130 Northern soldiers. The Southerners had evened the score from the previous day's battle.

Battery Wagner was safe, for the moment.

For the next week Union gunboats shelled Wagner daily. The bombardment was meant, in part, to provide cover for Northern troops who were busy building their own earthworks on Morris Island south of Battery Wagner. As a result of the barrage, the Confederates stayed safely behind the walls of the fort, which allowed the Union to prepare for the next assault. In the meantime the Yankees also attempted to distract the Southerners by plotting minor skirmishes on James Island. The idea was to prevent the Confederates from consolidating forces at Wagner.

The *Mercury* reported that little information had been gleaned from the prisoners of war taken in the most recent battle, but they had let slip one interesting fact: There were two Union regiments in South Carolina composed of black soldiers. The 2nd Regiment of South Carolina had been assembled earlier in the year by Col. James Montgomery. He enlisted free black citizens of South Carolina and escaped slaves, of whom there were many in the Lowcountry around Beaufort. Montgomery also found others less than willing to serve, so he conscripted them.

In June the 2nd Regiment had participated in a raid on Combahee Ferry, traveling with the escaped slave and famous abolitionist Harriet Tubman. The 2nd Regiment sailed from the St. Helena Sound up the Combahee River on one of three Union ships sent to drive the Confederates back. The Union troops burned several plantations and freed hundreds of South Carolina slaves. The 2nd Regiment would become more famous — or infamous, in the South — for burning and looting the town of Darien, a minor outpost on the Georgia coast. Southerners would cry foul over that attack, which had been ordered by Montgomery.

The 54th Massachusetts had been reluctant participants in the raid on Darien. Col. Robert Gould Shaw, the white commander of the 54th, reportedly called the raid a "Satanic action," but had little recourse to stop it. Montgomery was in charge and dismissed Shaw's protests. Darien never stood a chance. The 2nd Regiment was formidable enough, but the 54th was an even more elite fighting force. The 54th had been recruited and promoted by Massachusetts abolitionists, and enthusiasm for the regiment was so high that the Army had its pick of soldiers.

The presence of black troops in Charleston prompted Rhett to remind the *Mercury*'s readers of an order from Confederate President Jefferson Davis which said that any "negros (sic) or slaves" that made mutiny or insurrection, or rose in rebellion, would be tried and, in most cases, executed. While captured white soldiers could expect to end up in a prison camp, there was always the possibility of freedom through a prisoner exchange. Black soldiers did not have that option. If they were caught, the Southerners would kill them.

Still, the 54th Massachusetts officially announced its arrival on James Island on Thursday, July 16, with one of the Union's diversions. The regiment, trudging across the island before dawn, ran into a column of Southern infantry from Secessionville. The fight was short but brutal, and residents in downtown Charleston again heard

The men of the 54th Massachusetts and their fallen leader.

the gunfire. The Marion Artillery, the Chatham Light Artillery and the 25th Eutaw Regiment pushed the Northern troops all the way back to the Stono River. When it was over, more than a dozen men from the 54th had been captured.

Beauregard sent word of the capture of black troops to Richmond, asking if they should be turned over to state authorities "with the other negroes." The Confederates, at least in this instance, did not follow through with their threat. While some of the soldiers died as a result of wounds or the conditions in prisoner-of-war camps, many of those captured men from the 54th were eventually released at the war's end.

But the rest of the regiment did not know that at the time. And only two days passed before the Massachusetts soldiers got their shot at revenge.

On Friday, July 17, a Confederate soldier approached a woman selling peaches on King Street near the intersection of John Street. The private, who belonged to a regiment that had recently arrived in the city, forced the woman to give him some fruit

and refused to pay. A local boy, named by the *Mercury* only as "Rantin," berated the soldier for his behavior; when the boy turned to walk away, the soldier shot him with his musket. The ball went in one hip and out the other, a wound "of such a nature that the young lad is not expected to live." It was the beginning of a long, bloody weekend in Charleston.

On Saturday the heavy rain that had pelted the city for weeks ended, taking the excessive heat with it. Under a cloudless sky, a light breeze stirred the harbor. That morning Union guns began firing at Battery Wagner, an assault that went on for nearly three hours, lazy at first and then growing more intense that afternoon when five ironclads joined in the shelling. The *Mercury* would later report that the firing was so intense that "at one time, so rapid was the fire, that the reports averaged twenty-seven per minute."

Gen. Gillmore had thrown everything he had at Wagner in preparation for a night-time assault. He assumed the fort had been devastated by more than 10 hours of constant bombardment – an easy target for ground troops. But Rhett would later report that the damage to Fort Wagner was insignificant. The shelling would not taper off until dusk. And that's when the real assault began.

Just before 8 p.m., Confederate pickets spotted two columns of advancing Yankee troops. There were 3,000 men in each column, so many that there wasn't room on the beach for them all. Some were marching in seawater up to their knees. Gillmore had believed that an overwhelming show of force was all he needed to take the battery; after all, it had been a successful tactic at Fort Pulaski. He simply ordered his men to charge.

The Union troops moved quickly that night led by the men of the 54th Massachusetts. The 54th's column attacked on the right, bringing a direct assault at Battery Wagner. When they were 60 yards out, the Confederates stationed behind the parapet unleashed "a galling fire into the moving masses." But the 54th kept advancing.

While the second column found itself in the cross hairs of Fort Sumter's Dahlgren guns and Columbiads, the 54th conquered the moat protecting the battery, crossing the water and dodging the palmetto stakes. But when they reached the other side, Lt. Waties of Blake's Battery opened up with a raking fire from two brass howitzers that was soon "playing terrific havoc in the ranks of the assailants." The 54th was caught in the bloody repulse of a Confederate crossfire. Still, they kept coming.

Before long, the first troops from the 54th reached the Battery Wagner parapet. There they ran into heavy fire from the troops of the Charleston Battalion, a group of men who had seen action the previous summer at Secessionville. The 54th Massachusetts suffered heavy casualties. Col. Shaw, the commanding officer, was one of the first to fall, and many of his men soon fell by his side. But the rest continued to fight.

The battle lasted three hours and included two waves of assault from the 54th Massachusetts. It was nothing short of a Union bloodbath. The Confederates mowed down the enemy from behind Wagner's walls, a barrage that kept the Northern troops off balance the entire time. In the confusion some U.S. soldiers fell to friendly fire. Other Northern troops managed to storm one wall of Wagner left temporarily unmanned but were soon fighting hand-to-hand with Confederate troops. In the final hour of the fight, it was a battlefield of chaos.

"Men fell by scores on the parapet and rolled back into the ditch, many were drowned," one survivor later wrote, "and others smothered by their own dead and

Nearly 1,000 Union troops fell in the failed attack on Battery Wagner.

wounded companions falling upon them."

More than two hours into the battle, Brig. Gen. Johnson Hagood arrived with the 32nd Georgia, and his troops initially concentrated on those few Yankees that had made it inside the fort. The fight continued for almost another hour, the North's troops never able to gain the upper hand. By 11 p.m., the Union forces retreated.

The *Mercury* estimated that more than 1,500 Yankees died, and at least 200 — some of them members of the 54th — were taken captive. And when it was all over, the South still held Battery Wagner.

The Confederates' success on Morris Island restored a bit of confidence among Charleston residents, but the victory came with a heavy price. The Union Army had taken most of Morris Island and the Confederates still holding the northern tip were trapped with no way to replenish provisions – much as the Union troops at Fort Sumter had been before the war began. The clock was ticking for Battery Wagner.

The repercussions of the battle would be felt for the rest of the war. Although the 54th Massachusetts had suffered heavy casualties, the bravery and heroism of the black troops encouraged other free African Americans and former slaves to join the U.S. Army at a time when the South was desperate for new recruits. The odds in Charleston and across the South were quickly tilting more in favor of the Union.

The next day Confederate troops toiled under a July sun to bury the dead. As they worked, they must have wondered how long they, and Charleston, could hold out.

Union troops began shelling the Charleston peninsula in the early hours of Aug. 22, 1863, beginning the siege of Charleston.

CHAPTER 15

THE SIEGE

T he bodies were scattered over the dunes and scrub, contorted in unnatural positions, their faces frozen by the onset of rigor mortis.

As the sun rose over Morris Island on July 19, 1863, the Confederate defenders of Battery Wagner surveyed the ghastly remains of the previous night's battle. There were hundreds of bodies, most of them Union soldiers – men from Massachusetts, Connecticut, New York. Many of them had fallen in the moat protecting the fort, others were lying on the very edge of the battery and a few had come to rest in the surf, waves lapping against them. Some had been shot, others stabbed. The only thing all these dead men had in common was that they had taken their last breath from Southern air.

It had been a particularly vicious battle, perhaps the bloodiest in Charleston history. And most of that blood belonged to Union soldiers. The Confederates had shown once again that when faced with a must-win situation, they could prevail – even if the Union soldiers outnumbered them more than 2-to-1.

That morning the Confederate sentries spotted a white flag in the distance. The Yankees, it seemed, wanted a word. The Union soldiers who appeared outside the fort had been sent to request a cease-fire long enough for them to bury their dead. Battery Wagner officers did not consider the request for long before denying it. They assumed it was a trick, a ploy to allow Union officers to get a better look at the fort's defenses. For that reason the task of interment fell to Southern troops, who spent the entire day toiling in the Lowcountry sun. By nightfall, the *Mercury* reported — erroneously — that the Confederates had buried 600 men. The newspaper claimed the Yankees had buried another 200.

"Including those still unburied, and the wounded who have since died, the enemy's loss in killed alone must have been nearly or quite one thousand," the paper reported. "The number of prisoners taken by our troops (including wounded) was 276. Judging from these figures, and remembering the well-known habit which the Yankees have of carrying off their wounded, it seems quite reasonable to believe that their total loss in killed, wounded and prisoners could not have been less than two thousand."

The official estimate for Union casualties in the battle would be 1,500. Confederate casualties numbered 174. Some of those bodies would remain unburied when the fighting resumed the next day.

On Monday Union gunboats, including the *New Ironsides,* opened fire on Battery Wagner around 11 a.m., joined by land batteries that the Northern troops had constructed in the middle of the island. The firing continued unabated for more than an hour and a half with Wagner and Fort Sumter responding slowly, the *Mercury* reported. At Battery Wagner, four were killed and 11 were wounded before the boats were scared off.

"Fort Sumter got the range of the *Ironsides*, and little before four o'clock she withdrew," the paper reported the next morning. "The Monitors also hauled off, and for the remainder of the evening the firing was at long and irregular intervals, coming chiefly from the enemy's land batteries. Some shots were fired at Fort Johnson, and at the Shell Point battery."

Later the *Mercury* would offer intelligence that claimed the *New Ironsides* had been hit at least three times by Sumter shells, one of which fell on the warship's deck and convinced her officers to retreat. With some pride, *Mercury* editor Robert Barnwell Rhett Jr. relayed the news that some of the Yankee prisoners mentioned their distress at how accurate the guns of Sumter were.

The shelling resumed on Tuesday and continued intermittently through Wednesday, the shots thrown chiefly from two unidentified ironclads. It was clear that this was not merely the Union Navy going through the motions. This was a continuation of the assault begun earlier in the month. On Friday morning, a "cannonade far heavier than any that has been heard since Saturday last, was opened from the enemy's fleet and Morris Island batteries, against Battery Wagner," the *Mercury* reported. The *New Ironsides*, five Monitors and 19 other vessels steamed inside the bar and unleashed a barrage of fire.

According to the *Mercury*, "The bombardment, while it lasted, equaled in severity any which the defenders of Battery Wagner have thus far so gallantly sustained. Between six and seven o'clock the reports averaged fully twenty per minute, and, as the conflict proceeded, the harbor mists, dissipated by the rising sun, were succeeded by the heavy clouds of white smoke which went drifting from the scene of battle along the eastern horizon."

Although Battery Wagner fired back with enough intensity to show that this assault had not unnerved the Confederate forces there, it certainly left Charleston residents uneasy. The Yankees would not retreat; they would not give up.

The summer fell into a predictable pattern. Union warships and the Yankee guns on Morris Island would shell Battery Wagner for days, pause for one or two, and then resume the attack. Occasionally the Navy would turn its attention to Battery Gregg and the dunes around Cummings Point. The Confederates were sometimes slow to return fire, perhaps conserving ammunition, but the men at Sumter and Gregg each managed to hit the *New Ironsides* on July 30 before the day's engagement ended.

The Union had no intentions of giving up its plan to take Battery Wagner, but the purpose of these intermittent bombardments also served as a convenient decoy. Less than a week after taking the southern part of Morris Island, Northern commanders had brought in engineers to scout a location for a permanent battery. They needed to find some solid ground on the notoriously soft barrier island, capable of holding a tremendous weight. They walked the island until they finally found a satisfactory spot less than a mile from the highest ground on Morris Island. It was smaller than they had hoped but was a sturdy piece of land that lay between three creeks. There they would build a new battery, one that would prove particularly troublesome for Charleston.

At the same time Confederate troops were working furiously to improve the city's defenses. Beauregard himself inspected the works on James Island at the end of July and he must have been disturbed by what he found. The defenses were not up to the general's standards. At Beauregard's command, Confederate officials asked local planters to provide additional slaves to help reinforce local batteries.

Most plantation owners refused, claiming the military had already taken "as much negro labor as is requisite for the proper and energetic prosecution of the work upon our defences, and that, therefore, no more slaves are needed," the *Mercury* reported. Rhett took the planters to task, calling their refusal to help the cause "a grave mistake."

"A vast amount of work, of a very important character, remains to be accomplished, and there is still urgent need of as many negroes as the people of the state can supply for the emergency," the editor wrote. "The greater the number of hands furnished, the sooner will the necessary defences be completed and the negroes returned to their owners.... Let our planters, then, hasten to send down more negroes, while we have the opportunity to make their labor available. The fate of the city may turn upon the promptitude of the people of South Carolina in answering this last call of the authorities."

For the next few days the *Mercury* published pleas for locals to provide sandbags "for the protection of our harbor defences." The appeal was expanded to anyone who could "spare servants, either to fill the bags or to pull the boats as oarsmen." Of course, there was also a need for "experienced and competent overseers" to supervise the laborers.

"Besides this resource, the free colored men of Charleston might render important aid to the defence of the city by coming forward freely now and reporting themselves to the above-named gentlemen, to work either on the wharf or in the harbor," Rhett suggested. "They have always constituted a very respectable and orderly class in this community. Let them do their part now."

Rhett spoke for a large contingent of local residents clearly worried about the increased fighting along the coast. Each day brought more news of Union movement in the area. There had been more boats spotted in the Stono River, U.S. troops sneaking onto James Island, and then there was the increasing number of ships joining the blockading squadron. The Yankees had turned their full attention to the city.

On Aug. 4 Confederate troops ambushed a Yankee barge attempting to land more troops in the area. For several nights the Southerners had been aware of Yankee picket boats in Schooner Creek between James and Morris islands. These boats had lingered around the wreck of the old steamer *Manigault*, and it was assumed that these men were spying on Confederate movements around Cummings Point, or so the *Mercury* speculated.

Finally, on Tuesday night, the Confederates decided to act. Around 8:30, more

In the summer of 1863, Union forces would turn their guns on Fort Sumter, beginning the first major bombardment of the fort. Between Aug. 17 and Sept. 2, about 6,800 rounds would be fired at the fort.

than two-dozen men set out from Fort Johnson in rowboats while the ironclads *Chicora* and *Palmetto State* slipped into the creek. Capt. Sellers and the men of the 25th South Carolina Volunteers opted for stealth. They slid out of their boats and crept through the marsh, knee-deep in the muck. Before long, they came face to face with the Yankees.

The Union troops, taken by surprise, rushed to their boats in an attempt to escape. One barge got away but not without several casualties. The other boat was captured by Capt. Warley's men. Several men from the 100th New York Regiment were taken prisoners. The *Mercury* reported that the captain and four others were wounded, and two of the Union soldiers had been killed. The Southern casualties were limited to one: B. Furwick of Orangeburg, a member of Capt. Warley's unit.

The next day the prisoners were paraded through the city. The *Mercury* reprinted an article from the New York *Herald* that claimed Capt. Paine, one of the Union's best scouts, was among the captured. But the Confederates felt they had taken a bigger prize in the raid. One soldier used the parade to show off the captured field glasses of Gen. Gillmore. This might have boosted the morale of locals more if not for the sound of Union shells hitting Morris Island, a noise that was becoming all too common in Charleston.

Confederate President Jefferson Davis designated Friday, Aug. 21, a day of fasting, humiliation and prayer across the South. In response Rhett began his front-page editorial in the *Mercury* with a litany from the Book of Common Prayer: "In all time of our tribulation, in all time of our prosperity, in the hour of death, and in the day of judgment, good Lord deliver us." The Confederate States, Rhett wrote, "are now in trouble, and today has been set apart for the people to pray for deliverance from it as our Litany prescribes."

At least in Charleston, those prayers would go unanswered.

The Union forces spent much of the week furiously shelling Battery Wagner, beginning with a bombardment on Aug. 16 that the *Mercury* claimed was of unprecedented severity. Fort Sumter had repulsed a fleet of a dozen Yankee warships, but the vessels would not fall back for long. When they returned, the gunboats divided their attention between Wagner and Sumter. The best news Rhett could scrounge up was that no one at Sumter had been killed yet. Of course, the Yankees would not recognize Davis' call for a holiday. Heavy fire was directed at Sumter all that day. But the harshest blow came later that night.

Just before 11 p.m. a Union messenger delivered a letter to Battery Wagner. The dispatch from Brig. Gen. Q.A. Gillmore was addressed to Gen. Beauregard, and it was as chilling as it was blunt:

"I have the honor to demand of you the immediate evacuation of Morris Island and Fort Sumter, by Confederate forces. The present condition of Fort Sumter, and the rapid and progressive destruction which it is undergoing from my Batteries, seem to render its complete demolition, within a few hours, a matter of certainty. All my heaviest guns have not yet opened.

"Should you refuse compliance with this demand, or should I receive no reply thereto, within four hours after it is delivered into the hands of your subordinate at Fort Wagner, for transmission, I shall open fire on the city of Charleston from batteries already established, within easy and effective (range) of the heart of the city."

The Confederates had no way out. It was clear that Gillmore was not bluffing and had in fact set them up for failure. The note had been delivered to Morris Island; by the time a courier carried it to headquarters downtown there was no way to respond before the Union deadline passed. That was not even the worst of it: Beauregard was nowhere to be found. The general had set out to inspect field batteries in the countryside and his officers could not get word to him in time to plot a course of action.

They obviously would not give up their forts, but neither could they ignore Gillmore's demands and risk the deaths of civilians in Charleston. Without Beauregard to make a decision, the staff suffered a brief moment of panic before Thomas Jordan, chief of staff, had an idea. He would try to stall Gillmore.

Jordon, feigning outrage, sent the original letter back with his courier, along with a terse note: "This paper is returned for the signature of the writer."

Gillmore was not amused, and he wasted no time following through on his threat. At 1:30 a.m. on Aug. 22, the general gave the order and the Union's newest Morris Island battery fired a 150-pound projectile that soared nearly five miles over the harbor and landed on the city. It was the first of 16 shells that would rain down on the city that night. Charleston was under attack.

These shells were fired from the Marsh Battery, an earthworks fort designed by Northern engineers. Inside the battery, these men had built a platform capable of holding a massive, 8-inch Parrott gun that the Yankees affectionately called the Swamp Angel. It was capable of firing 150-pound rounds at least 7,900 yards, putting much of the city of Charleston within its range. If the Union could not take Sumter or Battery Wagner, they would simply bypass the forts. It was a turning point in the war: the Union was now targeting a civilian population, albeit one that mingled with various military targets.

Rhett would not give the Yankees the satisfaction of describing what, if any, panic there was in the streets of Charleston that night. The shells all landed on the lower portion of the peninsula among the finest homes south of the business district, but the *Mercury* claimed the projectiles did no damage. However, Rhett feigned outrage that the Lincolnites would fire on a city filled with innocent children and women.

"It is unnecessary to make any comments upon this act," Rhett wrote.

In fact, panic broke out when the first shell struck the city. There was no doubt this explosion was far closer than those that normally echoed across the harbor. One man who lived on The Battery ran to alert his neighbor, Williams Middleton. The plantation owner was asleep in his downtown home when a neighbor rousted him from his bed with the warning that the Yanks were shelling the city. Middleton, annoyed by the intrusion, nevertheless thanked the man and said all they could do was "let them shell and be damned."

At the Charleston Hotel, guests ran from their rooms after the first blast. The British artist Frank Vizetelly stepped into the hall to see dozens of people scampering around in their nightwear or less. "One perspiring individual of portly dimensions was trotting to and fro with one boot on and the other in his hand, and this was all the dress he could boast of," Vizetelly recalled. When another shell exploded in the city, the crowd dove at once to the floor. Vizetelly would spend the rest of the night in a saloon, wagering on where the next shot would hit.

For the rest of the weekend, the city would have no quiet. The *New Ironsides* and six other gunboats mercilessly assaulted Fort Sumter and Battery Wagner. Thousands of shells rained down on Fort Sumter, a barrage that knocked down its flag eight times, the *Mercury* claimed. Sumter and Moultrie fired back with gusto, allegedly hitting the *New Ironsides* once again. Meanwhile Confederate sharpshooters tried to take out the crews firing at the fort, to no avail. The trouble was that no one knew the source of the mysterious gun bombarding the city.

On Sunday the shooting began near midnight and stretched into the early morning hours. Shells came in 15-minute intervals, and there were between 14 and 18 of them. Rhett said most people believed the gun responsible for the attack on Charleston was hidden on Morris Island. "And there are yet others who declared that the obnoxious battery is a floating one, which the Yankees run up nightly under cover of darkness into one of the numerous creeks which intersect the neighboring islands," Rhett wrote. "It is to be hoped that the mystery will soon be solved and the battery silenced."

What no one in Charleston knew at the time was that the Swamp Angel was already out of commission. On Sunday evening the gun's breech had blown – an explosion that injured four men and sent the big gun flying off its carriage and into the parapet. In its brief career the Swamp Angel had fired only 36 shots at the city. Still, it would become a legend.

The Swamp Angel, an 8-inch Parrott rifle, lofted a 150-pound projectile into the city. Its career was short and actual damage to the city was slight. The Union battery was constructed over the marsh on a floating platform.

The loss of the fantastic gun was merely an inconvenience for the Union. The U.S. Army had other guns, and would soon replace the Swamp Angel. Eventually they would bring in guns with even greater range. The larger significance of the weekend bombardment was lost on no one in the city.

The siege of Charleston had begun, and it would be a long time before the city had any peace.

After months of shelling by Union troops on Morris Island and the blockade fleet, much of Fort Sumter was reduced to rubble. Still, the Confederates would not give up the fort.

CHAPTER 16

SUMTER STRIKES BACK

A tropical depression blew into the Lowcountry on Aug. 24, the wind gusting in intermittent bursts, the rain falling in torrents. The storm disrupted gunners from both the North and the South, forcing a brief – and increasingly rare – cease-fire in the siege of Charleston.

Before the bombardment resumed Tuesday morning, locals took advantage of clear skies to survey the damage from the weekend's battle, and it was far worse than anyone had imagined. Fort Sumter had been decimated. The *Mercury* reported that nearly 5,000 shells had been hurled at the fort over the weekend and estimated that three-quarters of them had been direct hits.

"It cannot be denied that the enemy fire with great accuracy," Robert Barnwell Rhett Jr. wrote. "The eastern face of the fort is now very seriously damaged, and almost every gun has been disabled."

While the men at Marsh Battery bombarded the city with the Swamp Angel, Sumter had been targeted by every other Union gun in the area. The fort was subjected to a lethal crossfire from Parrott guns on Morris Island and ironclads from the blockade. It was hit more than 700 times on Friday, and at least 600 shots struck it on Saturday. Throughout Sunday, 15-inch shells hammered Fort Sumter's walls, the brick crumbling under the destructive power of rifled guns.

"The south face is now but a heap of ruins," the *Mercury* reported, "and the west is cracked from top to bottom with supporting pillars shot away. Arches of the northwest face and terreplein have fallen in. The east face is cracked through and breached, the chief injury being at the level of the arches and terreplein. Our magazine has been partially penetrated by shell, and a shell room has also been perforated."

The Union was relentless. The shelling of Sumter and Battery Wagner continued throughout Tuesday, although at a slower pace than the North displayed over the weekend. The ironclads, struggling through the remnants of the tropical weather, were unable to join in the bombardment. It was small comfort to the Confederates at Sumter and Wagner, where the casualties mounted. News of the severe damage to Sumter trickled into the city throughout the week, prompting the *Mercury* to publish a premature obituary for the once-proud fort.

"Sumter is no longer a double-tiered battery," Rhett wrote. "As a great artillery fortress its proud proportions are reduced to ruins. But the ground is sacred to Southern independence. The site is negatively valuable, and, with even the rifle and bayonet only, it may be held still from the hands of our foes."

The Confederate troops had returned fire as best they could throughout the assault but there were too many targets and not enough working guns. The Southerners fought back through their exhaustion until they were relieved by less weary soldiers. But there was little relief to be had. It seemed to be a never-ending battle, their world permanently smoke-colored, their ears constantly ringing from the sound of explosives.

At Battery Wagner in particular, the men had little defense from the onslaught. One shell fell in front of an 8-inch gun, tore away the parapet and exploded in the gun chamber, killing two soldiers and wounding several others. Sgt. Welsh of the 1st S.C. Artillery noticed that an awning had caught fire, and tore it down. But he quickly realized the flames had ignited an ammunition barrel that had just been filled. Before the barrel could explode, Welsh calmly grabbed a pot of coffee and extinguished the fire.

"Such an act of heroism should not be left unchronicled or unappreciated," Rhett opined in the *Mercury.*

The Confederates remained under fire for the rest of the month, the intensity of the attack increasing each day. Then on Sept. 1 it appeared the Union fleet had moved in for the kill. The North's batteries on Morris Island fired nearly 400 shots at Sumter, 166 of which struck the outside walls and another 95 fell inside the fort, killing three soldiers. Sumter was unable to return fire but Battery Gregg, Fort Moultrie and the

Sullivan's Island guns defended it, fighting back with great spirit.

The *Palmetto State*, the *Chicora* and the city's new gunboat, the *Charleston,* took positions near the mouth of the harbor in case the Union ironclads attempted to run the gauntlet and reach the city. But the Union ships kept a safe distance, bombarding Sumter from afar and backed up by the guns of the *New Ironsides*. Sumter maintained its silence throughout the battle, its presence a dark shadow on the horizon. The *Mercury* reported that at least 100 Confederate shells hit Union ironclads as the battle ran into Sept. 2 "for five long hours, during which the harbor was filled with one grand diapason of artillery."

Then, to the surprise of the Southerners, the Union Navy ceased fire just before 5 a.m. and withdrew. The *Mercury* speculated at least one Yankee gunboat had been damaged in the attack, but could give no better reason for the retreat. The end of the battle marked the conclusion of what would become known as the first major bombardment of Fort Sumter. Between Aug. 17 and Sept. 2, the Union had fired an estimated 6,800 rounds at the fort, resulting in at least 52 casualties.

Sumter had been damaged irrevocably, but it was not yet finished.

All those Yankee ships.

They swung at anchor on the horizon, just out of the reach of Confederate guns, taunting Beauregard. They were the difference in the fight, he knew. The gunboats, particularly the dreaded *New Ironsides*, had shelled Sumter into submission. The Union batteries on Morris Island were relatively insignificant, certainly no match for the city's forts. If a few island guns were the only Northern presence in Charleston, it would be no contest. But the gunboats kept the Confederates distracted. And they inflicted much damage.

The Union had an excellent battle plan. Yankee gunboats steamed toward the shore, unloaded a barrage of shells on the forts and then retreated beyond the range of Southern guns. They were always moving targets, leaving Confederate gunners guessing and lucky to land a few shots now and then. The North was taking advantage of the South's greatest weakness. The Confederacy had gone to war without a Navy, and could not catch up. The *Palmetto State,* the *Chicora* and the *Charleston* were of little use. They were cumbersome and slow, and the *Palmetto State*'s engine had proven unreliable on occasion.

Beauregard realized that the fight would only grow more lopsided as time went on. The Union could bring in more boats, replacing them much more quickly than he could build new batteries. The general needed an edge. And finally, earlier that summer, he thought he'd found it.

A New Orleans engineer named James McClintock had recently completed work on a new kind of stealth boat, the third such vessel he had constructed. The first had been abandoned when New Orleans fell in April 1862 and the second was lost under tow in Mobile Bay. The first two boats had been financed by a Louisiana politician, a man Beauregard may have known. The third was built with money funded from various investors and seemed a dramatic improvement over the initial versions.

This machine – a "fish-boat," some called it – could travel beneath the water and deliver a killing blow to ships without ever being seen. It had been tested in Mobile Bay and proved quite effective, blowing an old hulking barge out of the water. Beauregard was intrigued, and knew he must have this weapon. Its talents were wasted in Mobile, which was too far from the open water to be in immediate danger.

Beauregard sent word to Confederate forces in Mobile, ordering the boat sent to Charleston immediately. Although the boat was not military property, the owners did not protest; in fact, they most likely welcomed the news. The only way to profit from this new machine was to sink blockade ships. There were rich Southern planters willing to pay up to $100,000 to any crew that could sink the infernal *New Ironsides* – and that ship was patrolling the waters off Charleston.

A crew in Mobile loaded the boat onto two train cars, draping it with canvas to hide its true shape. When it departed the general sent word along the route that nothing should slow the train's progress. It carried cargo that must arrive safely.

The fish-boat reached the John Street station on Aug. 15 just before the siege began, and it could not have inspired much confidence. It was simply a narrow iron tube, tapered at the ends, 40 feet long and barely five feet tall. The most distinguishing features on the contraption were two hatches on its top and two fins on its flanks. It did not look particularly menacing; in fact, it seemed unlikely the thing would even float.

The mechanics of the fish-boat were soon explained to Beauregard. Eight men operated the ship, seven of them dedicated solely to propulsion. These crewmen sat hunched over in the center compartment, which was roughly 42 inches wide, turning a crank that powered the boat's propeller. The captain sat up front, steering and

Union troops on Morris Island spent the summer shelling Fort Sumter.

operating the side fins, which controlled the depth at which the boat cruised. Ballast tanks at either end were filled with water to make the boat submerge; the water was expelled to allow it to surface.

The fish-boat attacked its prey with a simple floating contact mine. This powder keg was dragged behind the ship with a rope of at least 100 feet. The boat would dive below the surface and travel beneath the ship while pulling the mine into the side of its prey. When the device detonated, it would create a hole in the ship's hull large enough to sink it within minutes. The crews would never know what hit them.

McClintock arrived with the boat, but the engineer claimed it was a sensitive machine and its crew would need much practice before it was safe for offshore sailing. He recruited a group of local men and went about his work. For more than a week, locals saw the little boat slicing through the harbor between Forts Moultrie and Johnson, sometimes disappearing briefly. It rode so low in the water that even the swells could sometimes hide its presence.

Word of this strange new boat circulated through Charleston quickly, but Robert Barnwell Rhett Jr. wrote nothing about it in the pages of the *Mercury*. The newspaper was often complicit in war censorship, as Union soldiers sometimes managed to get copies of the paper. Beauregard meant for this new weapon to be a surprise and certainly didn't want the blockade fleet reading about it in the Charleston papers.

McClintock ran his tests for more than a week before the Confederates grew weary of waiting. As the *New Ironsides* and other Union gunboats had shelled Sumter to rubble, the engineer kept asking for patience. But by the end the month, military officials tired of McClintock's excuses. Confederate Gen. T.L. Clingman sent Beauregard word from Sullivan's Island that the secret weapon would not "render any service under its present management." McClintock was timid, Clingman said.

Within days, Beauregard seized the ship and turned it over to the Confederate Navy. Lt. John Payne, an officer on the *Chicora*, took command of the fish-boat project. Many of the sailors on the boat's crew were from the city's own ironclads, particularly the *Palmetto State*. Payne promised action quickly and made plans to attack the blockade on Saturday, Aug. 29 – just as the shelling reached its peak.

That evening, the crew boarded the boat at the Fort Johnson dock. They squeezed through the small hatches one by one, the low-profile of the boat rocking precariously as they stepped onto its hull. Payne, the captain, was the last to climb aboard. As he stepped into the forward hatch, the *Etiwan* steamed by. Later, witnesses would say that water from the *Etiwan*'s wake swamped the fish-boat, sending harbor water pouring into its two open hatches. That was enough to send the iron ship sinking to the bottom of the harbor.

Payne managed to jump away as the boat disappeared beneath him and the two men closest to each of the hatches managed to climb out, one of them – Charles Hasker – briefly trapped as the hatch closed on his leg. When Hasker broke the surface the crew of the *Chicora*, anchored nearby, pulled him from the water. The five remaining sailors were trapped inside as the fish-boat filled with water and settled on the muddy bottom 42 feet down. They did not survive.

The Confederates did not have the luxury of lingering on the catastrophe. The attack on Sumter was reaching its crescendo, and the South's secret weapon was lying at the bottom of the harbor, a useless iron tomb for five sailors. The *Mercury* made only scant mention of the incident – careful not to release details of the secret weapon – on Monday, Aug. 31, under the headline "Lamentable Accident."

"On Saturday last, Lieutenants Payne and Hasker were proceeding to make some experiments in the harbor. The boat, which contained a crew of nine men, unfortunately parted from its moorings and sank. Five of the crew were drowned."

As the first major bombardment of Fort Sumter neared its end, Beauregard was no closer to ridding himself of the *New Ironsides*, and the little fish-boat, which McClintock had called the *Hunley*, was lost. And with it, a little bit of the South's hope had sunk.

By the first week of September, the Confederates realized that Battery Wagner was lost. Southern troops at the fort had repelled the Union assault admirably, but it had cost them. The battery was low on provisions and drinking water – what little freshwater Morris Island held had been contaminated by the decomposing bodies buried in the sand. One Georgia soldier would later say that he no longer feared hell because "it can't touch Wagner."

Beauregard ordered a gradual withdrawal from the fort to reduce casualties, but the South would not get out without further bloodshed. At dawn on Friday, Sept. 4, sentries at Battery Wagner spotted a United States flag – "the hated flag of stars and stripes," the *Mercury* called it – flying from a Union earthwork that had been erected barely 150 yards from the fort. Within minutes, Union Parrott guns began shelling Wagner. Fifteen minutes later, the *New Ironsides* approached the island and joined in the assault.

For two and a half hours, the ship fired on the fort, killing at least two-dozen men from the 25th S.C. Volunteers. While the troops at Wagner scrambled to defend themselves, the Union land forces moved even closer to their position. The next afternoon U.S. land and sea forces trained all their guns on the battery. "This bombardment – beyond all doubt the most fierce and long continued which has taken place against Wagner since the beginning of the siege – lasted throughout Saturday and Saturday night, and did not abate until Sunday morning," the *Mercury* later reported.

Wagner was barely in any shape to defend itself, the Yankees chipping away at the last bit of resolve left in the troops. The shelling was too intense and lasted too long. Several Confederate batteries on James Island tried to protect the Morris Island fort, but their guns did little to deter the Union attackers. The Yankees lit up the entire harbor.

"It is almost impossible to describe the terrible beauty of the scene in Charleston harbor as witnessed on Saturday night from the city," Rhett wrote. "From Moultrie almost to Secessionville, a whole semi-circle of the horizon was lit up by incessant flashes from cannon and shell. As peal on peal of artillery rolled across the waters, one could scarcely resist the belief that not less than a thousand great guns were in action.

"It was a grand chorus of hell," the *Mercury* editor said.

By Sunday more than 150 Confederate troops on Morris Island were dead, and the Union still wasn't finished. The shelling resumed again that evening. Col. L.M. Keitt, who commanded the Southern forces on Morris, had sent word to headquarters earlier in the day that he had only about 400 men able to fight. If there was no order to evacuate, Keitt said, he would rather launch an assault on the Union troops on the island rather than sit there and be shelled into submission. But Beauregard didn't want any more casualties. At 6 p.m. Keitt received orders to abandon Batteries Wagner and Gregg.

They would leave under the cover of darkness. As the incoming fire continued, the Confederates made their final preparations. They buried their dead as best they could and spiked the battery's guns – much as Anderson's men had done before evacuating Fort Moultrie. By nightfall, the healthy troops were carrying the wounded to barges that would ferry them to Fort Johnson. There were so many incapacitated Southerners that it took 40 barges to move them all.

Around 1 a.m. Keitt and his officers boarded the last barge and left Battery Wagner for the final time. As they sailed away, ceding the entirety of Morris Island to U.S. forces, they must have remembered a prediction made a year earlier: If Wagner falls, Sumter falls. And if Sumter falls, Charleston falls.

The Union had every intention of proving that prediction true. Shortly after occupying Battery Wagner, Northern troops began making plans to take the beleaguered Fort Sumter. At first, they tried the direct approach. Union Admiral John Dahlgren sent word to Confederate Maj. Stephen Elliott, the new commander at Sumter, that he should simply hand over the fort as it was in no shape to defend itself. Elliott was defiant in his reply.

"Inform Admiral Dahlgren that he may have Fort Sumter when he can take it and hold it," Elliott said.

The lines had been drawn. For several nights after that the Union sent scout barges close to the fort on reconnaissance missions. They were studying Sumter, collecting details for a different sort of attack on the fort. But someone made a fatal mistake: Dahlgren's orders fell into Southern hands. These notes, which were eventually published in the *Mercury*, called for 200 volunteers for "special service" aboard barges that would sail inside the Charleston bar. The Yankees were actually going to try to land on Fort Sumter and take it in hand-to-hand combat.

Armed with this intelligence, the Confederates watched every move of these reconnaissance troops, waiting patiently for them to come into range of their guns. When the attack came at 1:30 a.m. on Sept. 9, it was no surprise. The sentries spotted a convoy of barges that was half a mile long. Each boat carried 50 or more men, and they were headed for the rocks at the base of the fort's seaward face.

"As soon as the barges were seen by our vigilant sentries on the parapet, three rockets were thrown up to notify their comrades at the other batteries of the danger at hand," the *Mercury* later reported.

The sailors Dahlgren had assembled assumed there would be only a "corporal's guard" at the fort, easy pickings for 500 armed Union combatants. Instead they were met with the full might of the Confederate military. Fort Johnson, Battery Simkins, Fort Moultrie and the nearby *Chicora* immediately opened fire on the barges. The closest boats reached the rocks without being hit, however, and the troops aboard sprang ashore.

And there they met Maj. Blake's Charleston Battalion.

The Northern troops quickly realized they had fallen into a trap. The barges at the rear of the line had already turned and escaped. But those closest to the fort were stopped. The Union troops who had already landed tried to put up a fight but were quickly overpowered. Within minutes, the Confederates took more than 100 prisoners. The battle was over.

Dahlgren had overplayed his hand and Beauregard outfoxed him by installing infantry at the fort. It was a serious miscalculation for the Union and would ensure that the key to Charleston Harbor would remain out of reach for some time. The Confederates were hard at work restoring their firepower and would be even better prepared the next time the Yankees called on them. The blockading squadron got the message.

Fort Sumter was not yet finished.

The USS *New Ironsides* was the bane of Charleston's existence throughout the Civil War. The blockader was arguably the most powerful ship guarding the harbor entrance and unmercifully shelled Fort Sumter. The Confederates employed the use of several stealth boats in hopes of taking out the tough ship. Photo courtesy of the Library of Congress.

CHAPTER 17

A PRESIDENTIAL VISIT

The little boat slipped out of Charleston Harbor just after dark, hugging the edge of the channel. It was practically invisible from a distance and even at close range made for a puzzling sight: the boat looked very much like the flank of a whale bobbing on the surface. The only thing that ruined the illusion was its tall, thin smokestack. Just aft of that stack, Lt. William T. Glassell watched for troublesome Yankee gunboats as he scanned the horizon for his target: the USS *New Ironsides.*

This strange craft was called the *David,* the Biblical allusion intentional. It was cigar-shaped, just over 50 feet long and not even six feet wide. Designed by two Charleston men, Theodore D. Stoney and Dr. St. Julien Ravenel, the tiny torpedo boat had been built for stealth. In addition to its low profile, the boat's engine burned anthracite coal, which produced a colorless smoke. The ship was meant to sneak into the blockade line and plant charges in the hulls of much larger warships.

Gen. Beauregard had been intrigued by the design and thought this craft seemed infinitely more practical than the fish-boat *Hunley.* The *David* simply rode low in the water; it did not attempt to submerge. There were six of these torpedo boats under construction, each equipped with a deadly ramming spar designed by Francis D. Lee. This night, Oct. 5, 1863, would be the first real test of both boat and spar.

The *New Ironsides* most definitely qualified as the *David*'s Goliath. The warship had come to represent the might of the U.S. Navy. The 230-foot, armor-plated ship — powered by steam and sail — carried more than a dozen powerful guns, weapons

The *David* was a low-profile torpedo boat designed and built locally to take out blockade ships. This *David*, photographed after the war, was one of several allegedly used by Confederates and may be the one that attacked the *New Ironsides* in October 1863.

it had used with great efficiency against Fort Sumter and Battery Wagner. Most people in Charleston simply called the ship the "Ironsides" in a tone that conveyed both respect and disdain. They believed that sinking this ship could inflict serious damage on the Yankees' morale, and improve their own.

It took about an hour for the *David* to get across the bar. Just after 9 p.m. Glassell spotted the *New Ironsides* swinging at anchor off Morris Island. There were few other boats around it, which was good. The torpedo boat crept along for a while, but when the *David* was less than a mile away Glassell ordered the crew to speed up. The cigar boat sliced through the water making 7 mph and reached the *New Ironsides*' flank just as someone on the mighty ship's deck spotted it.

The gunfight began immediately. Deckhands began shooting down at the little boat and Glassell popped up and returned fire using all he had available: buckshot. Still, he somehow managed to hit one of the officers on deck. In the midst of this awkward battle, the *David* rammed the *New Ironsides* directly amidships. The explosion was immediate, loud and came with an unforeseen side effect.

The blast threw a thick wall of seawater into the air that rained down hard on the *David*. So much water fell into the boat's smokestack that it immediately extinguished the fire in its boiler. All of a sudden, the torpedo boat was powerless, adrift within easy range of the *New Ironsides*' considerable guns. The ship's crew had been disoriented by the explosion but recovered quickly. A few grabbed rifles and fired at the torpedo boat as it drifted out of sight.

While the *David* casually rocked in the dark swells, Glassell worried. He feared that the *New Ironsides* would slip its anchor and come looking for his boat – and eventually blow it out of the water. The torpedo boat's one flaw was that it got only one chance to deliver a killing blow. If it failed, the *David* was certainly no match for any armed ship. Considering all of this, Glassell finally, and reluctantly, gave the order to abandon ship. The four men jumped into the cold, inky water and prayed the tides would carry them to shore.

None of the men were in the water long. Glassell and another crewman, Sullivan, were soon picked up by a passing blockade ship and taken prisoner. But the *David's* engineer, J.H. Tombs, did not swim far from the torpedo boat before turning back. Tombs saw little advantage in swimming alone in the open ocean. He would take his chances aboard the boat. He found J.W. Cannon – the boat's navigator – clinging to the smoke stack.

Cannon had also recognized the long odds: He might die if a blockade ship found the boat, but he would certainly perish if he jumped in the water because he could not swim. Tombs took control of the situation and together the two men worked furiously, and eventually they managed to restart the boiler fire. As the blockade ships began to swarm, the *David* stealthily slipped away.

It wasn't a perfect attack by any stretch of the imagination, but the *David* had injured the *New Ironsides*. For the moment, at least, it appeared that Charleston might have a new secret weapon.

It would be days before the city learned of the attack outside the harbor. On Oct. 7 the *Mercury* gave a brief mention of the encounter, continuing its policy of divulging little information about the Confederacy's secret weapons. Robert Barnwell Rhett Jr. did his best to sound upbeat, but his disappointment in the battle's outcome was barely concealed.

"The small hours of Tuesday morning were marked by a very gallant and encouraging, though only partially successful, attack on the enemy's fleet. Of the character or details of the attacking expedition we deem it best for the present to be silent, and we are requested by the military authorities to extend to the Southern newspapers elsewhere the request to omit all mention of any definite intelligence that may reach them in reference to the affair. We can only inform readers that the Yankee ironclad frigate *Ironsides* is believed to have been injured, though she still rode at her usual anchorage yesterday afternoon."

Within a few days the city would learn that the *New Ironsides* had not suffered as much damage as the Southerners hoped. On Saturday, Oct. 10, the crew of a local mail boat spotted two U.S. soldiers in a small craft — guns in hand, field glasses held to their eyes. They appeared to be spying on Fort Sumter. The men on the mail boat, which carried dispatches between the city and Sumter, were "wholly unarmed" but knew they must do something to stop the Yankees. So they decided to bluff.

The mailmen "called out lustily to the occupants of the small boat to pull alongside and surrender," the *Mercury* later reported. Although the Union men were armed and wearing U.S. Army uniforms, they apparently had no appetite for a gunfight. They quickly surrendered and tried to muddle through an excuse, claiming they had mistaken Fort Sumter for the *New Ironsides* in the darkness.

The two Union soldiers turned out to be more competent spies for the South than their own side. Shortly after they were locked up in the city jail, the men began to talk and would not stop. They told their captors about the Union's latest movements off Charleston, and then claimed the attack on the *New Ironsides* was a failure. The torpedo boat had inflicted little damage on the great warship, the Yankees said, and confirmed that Glassell and Sullivan were now prisoners aboard one of the blockade ships.

They saved the most ominous news for last. The soldiers said Robert Parker Parrott, inventor of the famous gun, had been on Morris Island for more than a week helping the troops prepare for a new bombardment of Charleston. The North had several 300-pounders, these Yankee spies claimed, which could fire six miles – putting the city well within their range. This was not welcome news among local residents, especially when a massive explosion rocked the peninsula that same day.

But it was not an attack. A group of young boys had been playing with an unexploded Yankee shell and accidentally detonated it. They found the round at the ammunition storehouse on Southern Wharf, near Gen. Ripley's headquarters. One of the children thrust a heated wire into the shell, and that worked as well as any fuse. In the blast two boys and a slave were killed, their bodies charred beyond recognition. The *Mercury* called it an accident caused by carelessness, one that could have been avoided through "ordinary precautionary measures."

The incident distracted the city for a moment, but no one could forget the more pressing news delivered by the two Union prisoners: The city would be shelled again, and soon.

For the first half of October the Union troops on Morris Island were eerily quiet. The Southerners could see that the Yanks were busy at work on something at Cummings Point and knew from Northern prisoners that they were preparing to resume the bombardment from Marsh Battery. The focus of the men in blue was intense. Not even shelling from Confederate batteries that was "more rapid and regular than usual" could entice the Yankees into a fight.

The Confederates were also making preparations, albeit none that would appear in the paper. On Thursday, Oct. 15, the biggest news of the day would occur just a few blocks from the *Mercury* office, but Rhett would make no mention of it in print. The fish-boat was about to launch once again.

The submarine had been recovered from the harbor in September but only because the Confederate military wanted to give the men who had died in it a proper burial. Divers wrapped chains around the fish-boat and had a ship pull it from the muck. Then workers went about the grisly work of removing the bodies. After sitting in the water for days, the five men were so bloated that they had to be cut into pieces to remove them from their iron coffin.

Beauregard had been inclined to let the *Hunley* rot after the remains of his sailors were retrieved, but he soon had a run-in with the sub's namesake. Horace Hunley had arrived in the city, discovered what had happened to the boat and demanded it be returned to him immediately. Since the Confederates saw no future for the craft, they had no qualms about granting his wish.

Hunley argued that the fish-boat worked perfectly, that Beauregard had erred in letting men with no experience operate it. He brought in men from Mobile, Ala., who had worked on its construction to serve as a new crew. They scrubbed the hull, made sure it was in perfect order and, by mid-October, were ready to demonstrate that the sub could effectively attack the blockade.

It was a dreary morning. A drizzle left the air thick with a haze that hung over the harbor, enveloping the small crowd that had gathered at Adger's Wharf to watch Hunley test his boat. Most people in Charleston knew about the sub. If they hadn't seen it arrive at the train station or watched it cross the harbor, they had at least heard of it – particularly after it sank at Fort Johnson.

Although he had financed the two previous submarines built by James McClintock, and had this one named for him, Horace Hunley had nothing to do with the design of the fish-boat. He was a lawyer, a politician and an idea man. The mechanics meant little to him. None of that dampened his confidence, however. Hunley believed he understood the concept of the sub well enough to command it. The men from Mobile could handle the rest, he assumed. As usual, he didn't concern himself with trifling details.

The politician proved to be something of a showman. After the seven crewmen climbed into the submarine, Hunley paused. He pointed across the harbor to the *Indian Chief*, a Confederate receiving ship that would serve as his target. Hunley was calling his shot for the assembled crowd, letting them know he would dive under the ship and surface on the other side. After that he disappeared into the sub's forward hatch.

The *Hunley* pulled away from the dock moments later, cutting through the dark water silently as the crowd on the wharf watched it churn through the swells. As it approached the *Indian Chief* anchored in the Cooper River, the fish-boat slowly submerged. The people on shore waited, and the crew of the receiving ship watched the water for several tense minutes. And then, nothing. The fish-boat never surfaced.

Weeks later, divers found the sub 60 feet down. Chains were attached to the boat and it was dragged to shore at Mount Pleasant. When crews opened the boat and surveyed the scene inside, they concluded the accident was caused by pilot error. Horace Hunley had opened the valve that allowed water to flow into the boat's forward ballast tank so that it would submerge – but he never shut it off. The tiny crew compartment had filled with water, drowning the men from Mobile as quickly as the *Hunley* buried itself bow first in the harbor floor.

Hunley was found with his head in the forward conning tower, the last remaining pocket of air in the sub, clutching a candle. He had forgotten his last detail.

The *Mercury* obeyed Beauregard's order to ignore the accident. But on Friday, Oct. 16, the Charleston *Daily Courier* ran a small notice of the accident on its front page. The story carried the headline "Melancholy Occurrence" and was vague enough to avoid raising the general's ire.

"On Thursday morning an accident occurred to a small boat in the Cooper river, containing eight persons, all of whom were drowned: Their names were Captain Hunly (sic), Brockbank, Park, Marshall, Beard, Patterson, McHugh and Sprague, Their bodies, we believe, have all been recovered."

Their bodies actually would not be recovered for two weeks, but that was a detail the newspaper omitted. The *Courier* was also a willing accomplice in war censorship. To admit the bodies had not been recovered would only raise uncomfortable questions about the craft, and they did not want to raise the suspicions of Northern soldiers who managed to find copies of the paper. When the *Hunley* was finally brought ashore in early November, the papers scarcely bothered to mention it. Charleston had other things on its mind. By then the Union had broken its long silence.

At 10:30 on the morning of Oct. 26, the guns of Batteries Wagner and Gregg roared to life for the first time in nearly two months. Shells rained down on Fort Sumter and Sullivan's Island until dark. The Union had finally turned the South's own guns against it, a barrage that would not end for days. By Wednesday, the 28th, the *Mercury* reported that 670 shots had been fired at Sumter, only 88 of which missed their mark. Early the next day, 117 shots were fired at Sumter, all but seven hitting the fort. Most of the other shots apparently were meant to take out the bridge connecting Sullivan's to the mainland, but the Yankees couldn't hit it.

All of this, of course, was part of the Union's overall plan to take Charleston. The *Mercury*, recounting reports out of the Philadelphia *Inquirer*, said that once Sumter was reduced to rubble, the blockade fleet would steam into the harbor and take the city. Rhett offered this news matter of factly, also noting that only four shots had been fired into the city that week. Just one of those landed on the peninsula – slicing through an unoccupied house without doing much damage.

Life went on in Charleston. On Thursday night, J.J. Fickling reported that a black

A Confederate photographer took this interior photo of Fort Sumter in 1864. The fort had been decimated by near-continuous shelling by Union batteries and gunships. Note the two soldiers in the center background. Library of Congress photo

man climbed his fence with the intention of stealing some of his chickens. When Fickling tried to stop the man, he was stabbed in the head, neck and left arm. The assailant escaped, unidentified. On Saturday the Soldiers Relief Association made plans to deliver cooked meals to men at several harbor forts, and the Circular Church announced plans to hold Sunday services in the lecture room of the Third Presbyterian Church. Such were the lingering inconveniences of the Great Fire.

The rest of the city spent the weekend preoccupied with the pending presidential visit. Jefferson Davis, en route to Richmond after visiting Mobile, had decided to call on Savannah and Charleston. Rhett noted it was Davis' first visit to the city since the Confederacy had been formed, and the city's remaining residents did their best to make the city hospitable for the president.

As the train carrying Davis and his distinguished guests passed through the Lowcountry on Monday, Nov. 2, Confederate soldiers lined the tracks to cheer it on. The train stopped briefly at Pocotaligo and Adams' Run, and Davis used both occasions to greet the troops. When the train finally reached the depot on John Street, Beauregard was waiting to offer the president a carriage ride into the city. The pomp and circumstance delighted many of the Charlestonians lining their route, but it was purely a show for the masses. Beauregard and Davis largely despised each other.

Brig. Gen. P. G. T. Beauregard

The procession moved slowly toward downtown, a circuitous route that included Spring, Rutledge, Calhoun and Meeting streets before finally arriving at City Hall. Locals crowded the sidewalks along the route, the *Mercury* said, for a brief glimpse of "the chief magistrate of the Confederacy." At the corner of Broad and Meeting, local women had hung garland and a wreath that included a banner: "Ladies of the Soldiers' Relief Association welcome President Davis to Charleston."

Mayor Macbeth and the city council received Davis on the City Hall portico, where the president delivered some brief remarks to the crowd after a band played "Hail to the Chief." He noted that the city had changed dramatically since his last visit, an unhappy reminder of the city's condition following fires and the ongoing siege. Davis recovered quickly by playing to the crowd — invoking the name of John C. Calhoun and calling him the champion of states' rights in a "glowing tribute."

As Davis spoke the thunderous sound of Yankee guns echoed across the harbor, nearly drowning out his voice. Unable to ignore the barrage, the president was prompted to say that if the city ever became a prize of the foe, he hoped it would only "be as a mass of ruins." It was perhaps not the best thing he could have said – another

Confederate President Jefferson Davis made his first and only presidential visit to Charleston on Nov. 2, 1863. He stayed for several days, touring harbor defenses with Gen. P.G.T. Beauregard, with whom he had a somewhat strained relationship.

reminder of Charleston's charred and crumbling façade. Forced to recant once again, Davis assured the crowd that he did not think that would happen. He predicted any Union forces who attempted to take this city would meet a disastrous defeat.

Davis spent most of the week in Charleston, staying at former Gov. William Aiken's house on Elizabeth Street. He attended receptions in his honor and spent his days touring harbor defenses. On Tuesday he traveled to Sullivan's Island, where he visited Fort Moultrie and some of the batteries. The *Mercury* reported that "his Excellency expressed himself highly pleased" with what he found. Later, the president boarded one of the local ironclads – most likely the *Palmetto State* – to get a closer look at the "ruins of Fort Sumter." And on Wednesday, Davis was on James Island to review the troops at Fort Johnson, Secessionville and Fort Lamar.

At 7:30 on Thursday morning, Beauregard, Ripley and Jordan were on hand as Davis was escorted from Gov. Aiken's house by the Charleston Light Dragoons and Dunovant's regiment. They led the president to the depot, where he boarded a train north with plans to stop in Wilmington for a couple of days before returning to the capital. Rhett, whose father had opposed Davis' candidacy, waited until the president was safely out of town before delivering a sly insult disguised as a compliment.

"President Davis looks remarkably well – much more hearty than when elected to his office," the *Mercury* reported.

As the train pulled away from the depot that morning the Union was shelling Fort Sumter – a barrage that would continue, off and on, for another month. Despite the president's assurances, he left the people of Charleston wondering when – not if – the Yankees guns would once again turn on the city.

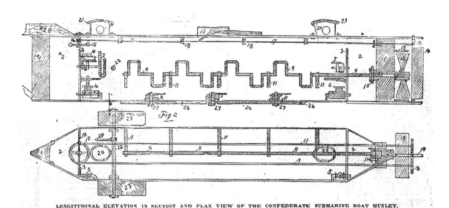

LONGITUDINAL ELEVATION IN SECTION AND PLAN VIEW OF THE CONFEDERATE SUBMARINE BOAT HUNLEY.

From Sketches by W. A. Alexander.

No. 1. The Bow and Stern Castings. No. 2. Water ballast tanks. No. 3. Tank bulkheads. No. 4. Compass. No. 5. Sea cocks. No. 6. Pumps. No. 7. Mercury gauge. No. 8. Keel ballast stuffing boxes. No. 9. Propeller shaft and cranks. No. 10. Stern bearing and gland. No. 11. Shaft braces. No. 12. Propeller. No. 13. Wrought ring around propeller. No. 14. Rudder. No. 15. Steering wheel. No. 16. Steering lever. No. 17. Steering rods. No. 18. Rod braces. No. 19. Air box. No. 20. Hatchways. No. 21. Hatch covers. No. 22. Shaft of side fins. No. 23. Cast-iron keel ballast. No. 27. Bolts. No. 28. Butt end of torpedo boom. No. 23. Side fins. No. 24. Shaft lever. No. 25. One of the crew turning propeller shaft. No. 31. Keel ballast.

Design sketches of the *H.L. Hunley.*

CHAPTER 18

FISH-BOAT

The procession marched into Magnolia Cemetery at 4 p.m. on Nov. 8, winding its way through tombstones and live oaks until it reached a spot near the back of the grounds. An honor guard carried the wooden casket, followed by the Rev. W.B. Gates, a military escort and a surprising number of locals. The group moved slowly, wandering past monuments to some of Charleston's most noted families before finally stopping at a shaded plot not far from the river – a symbolic location, perhaps.

These military funerals were a ritual that had become all too common in Charleston. On this Sunday the deceased was Horace Lawson Hunley, who had been fished out of his boat the day before. It had taken three weeks to find and raise his namesake sub from the depths of the Cooper River. When Gen. Beauregard finally saw the blackened face of Hunley's corpse, he was so disturbed by the sight that he ordered a military funeral for the Louisiana man – even though he was decidedly civilian.

Gardner Smith, a friend of Hunley's who had been summoned to the city only to arrive three days after the accident, later called the ceremony solemn and impressive. Smith clipped a lock of Hunley's hair and sent it, along with his waterlogged pocket watch, to Volumnia Hunley Barrow, the captain's sister. In his letter to Barrow, he said that during the service he could not refrain from tears.

The *Mercury*, which had not reported the full circumstances of Hunley's death, nonetheless carried the story of his funeral prominently under the headline "Last Honors To A Devoted Patriot."

"Possessed of an ample fortune, in the prime of his manhood — for he was only thirty-six at the time of his death — with everything before him to make life attractive, he came to Charleston, and voluntarily joined in a patriotic enterprise which promised success, but which was attended with great peril," Robert Barnwell Rhett Jr. wrote. "Though feeling, as appears from the last letter which he wrote to his friends, a presentiment that he would perish in the adventure, he gave his whole heart, undeterred by the foreboding, to the undertaking, declaring that he would gladly sacrifice his life in the cause. That presentiment has been mournfully fulfilled."

Rhett could be forgiven his melancholy, for it accurately reflected the mood of Charleston in the fall of 1863. The siege was now into its 121st day, the Yankees becoming more viciously efficient each week. Union troops on Morris Island and at Cummings Point shelled Sumter almost daily, reducing the fort to further ruin. There seemed to be no break in sight, no way to stop the relentless attack.

Soon, the Northern forces expanded their range to Fort Moultrie, firing on the Sullivan's Island outpost "with considerable severity" by the week's end. The *Mercury* could do little but report the number of shells that fell each day and tally the Confederates killed in the bombardments. It was depressing but by Thanksgiving Rhett had rallied enough to strike an upbeat tone in his holiday message to the city.

"While our great Cause has not prospered as we had hoped and desired, still it is strong and full of life." Although the city had again become a target of shelling, Rhett sarcastically noted that, "It will please the Yankees to know that no one was hurt."

In truth, the city was dying. The lower peninsula, which took the brunt of the shelling, was nearly deserted save for Southern soldiers who had nowhere else to camp. Businesses had finally fallen victim to nearly three years of war. At the end of the month, the Charleston Hotel announced it was closing. The *Mercury* tried to blame the death of the hotel's proprietor but was forced to report that the Mills House was considering similar action. Every day more bad news arrived, accompanied by the sound of cannon fire.

Charleston residents, the ones who remained, had to wonder how much longer they could take this.

On Sunday, Dec. 6, troops at Fort Sumter watched the *New Ironsides* lower its boats in a nasty gale. Fighting formidable waves, the boats made their way toward Morris Island, quickly disappearing in the haze. The Confederates feared the worst, but there was no firing from the island all day. In fact, the second major assault on Sumter had ended, although it would take Southern troops several days to realize this. And more than a week would pass before they understood the purpose of the dangerous maneuvers carried out by the *New Ironsides'* boats.

It had all happened suddenly. That afternoon the ironclad USS *Weehawken* sent up its distress flag in the midst of the gathering storm. The ship, which had been damaged by shelling two months before when it ran aground off Morris Island, was now in trouble again. The ironclad was taking on water in the rough weather and its bilge pumps, filled with debris, could not work fast enough to stop the seawater pouring into the hull. The *Weehawken* was foundering.

The crew tried to beach the boat, but it was sluggish and unresponsive – it had taken on too much water. There was no way to make it to the safety of shallow water off Morris. Within minutes of discovering the trouble, the Passaic-class Monitor's bow dipped beneath the wave and its stern lifted into the air. The *Weehawken* was going down.

Some of the crew managed to climb out in time and were rescued by the *New Ironsides'* lifeboats. But at least 30 men rode the gunboat to the Atlantic floor, where it would serve as their tomb. The Confederates took little satisfaction from the news when the city finally learned what had happened. Two months earlier they had failed to sink the ironclad when it was stuck within easy range of their guns. The weather proved more effective than Southern firepower.

The *Weehawken*'s sinking proved to be only the first bizarre incident of 1863's final month. Before Charleston learned of the ironclad's fate, Fort Sumter suffered a similarly strange and unexplained accident. On the morning of Dec. 11, troops at the fort were enjoying a rare break from the Yankee shelling and a brief respite from the weather. Many of the soldiers took advantage of the conditions to get their rations from the commissary. A line formed.

The explosion came out of nowhere: a loud report followed by an instant – and intense – fire. Sumter was burning, the blaze so massive that it was spotted by some people on The Battery. A small arms magazine next to the commissary had blown up, instantly killing the commissary officer, his men and the first several soldiers in line. The concussion of the blast knocked many others to the ground.

No one would ever know for certain what caused the explosion, perhaps because all the evidence was incinerated. The magazine burned uncontrollably for a while, the troops powerless to extinguish the blaze. When lookouts on the blockade ships spotted the smoke pouring out of the fort, the U.S. Navy took advantage of the situation, shelling Sumter mercilessly. In the confusion, several soldiers finally were able to block all passageways to the magazine, suffocating the fire. By then the damage had been done: at least 80 men were injured and 10 were dead, including Capt. Frost, Sgt. Swanson and three members of Capt. Gaillard's company.

"The strength of the fort is by no means impaired by the accident," the *Mercury* reported. "The resistive power is still as strong as usual, and the confidence of the garrison remains unshaken."

It was a sly bit of propaganda on Rhett's part, aimed directly at blockading fleet officers who often managed to get copies of the paper. In fact, much of the fort was out of commission as a result of the blast. If the Union launched an assault in the days after the explosion, the Confederates at Sumter knew they would be finished.

At 1 a.m. on Christmas morning, the Union troops on Morris Island sent Charleston a most unappreciated gift. The island batteries erupted, opening fire on the city when residents least expected it.

"For hours before the eastern sky was streaked with the first gray tints of morning, the cold night air was rent by other sounds than the joyous peals from the belfry and the exploding crackers of exhilarated boys," the *Mercury* reported. It was a shelling more severe than on any other occasion as five guns — three at Battery Gregg, one at Cummings Point and another at Mortar Battery — fired so relentlessly that sometimes three shells struck the city simultaneously.

"Several houses were struck," the paper reported, "but most buried themselves harmlessly in the earth."

In less than 12 hours Union guns hurled 134 shells at the city, leading to at least two casualties. William McKnighton, 83, was sitting by the fireplace in his downtown home when a shell burst through the wall, taking off his right leg. Shrapnel from the impact crushed his sister-in-law's foot. Both managed to survive.

For the next week there would be no holiday from the war. The bombardment continued intermittently until New Year's Eve when, just after sunset, the Union fired two shots at Sumter. When the fort returned fire, the Northern troops dipped their flag in respect. It was a rare display of courtesy from the Yankees.

Although the troops at Fort Sumter had every right to be demoralized, some of them merely accepted their plight as life during the war. One soldier, Henry Bentivoglio Middleton, even managed to sound cheerful in letters to his family. The former Citadel cadet wrote to his uncle – Williams Middleton, owner of Middleton Place – that Christmas had been dull at Sumter, an amazingly nonchalant characterization. He described "the magnificent ruins of the Fort, almost comparable to the Colosseum," and said that sitting on gun duty late at night it was "dreadfully cold here. The wind rushes in from all sides." Still, Middleton called his time at the fort a "good stretch."

Few in Charleston were as upbeat as young Middleton, for they had lived through the siege far longer. The darkest days of the war had set in, and Rhett for the first time was forced to broach the possibility that the South might lose the war. It was a future, he noted, of "subjugation."

"Try to imagine the scenes which would take place all over this country on the first day of acknowledged subjugation — that is, the day which should witness a treaty for reconstruction upon any terms whatsoever. From that moment, the right name of this war would be rebellion; and, what is more to the purpose, as rebels its ringleaders would be punished and its soldiers disarmed. Our Confederate flag, that has blazed in front of twenty pitched battles, would be formally lowered, officially torn, trampled, and abolished forever, while the accursed Stars and Stripes would be proudly hoisted in its place, upon every fort and in every camp, with cannon thunders and Yankee cheers."

It was a future of shame, Rhett speculated, one that Charleston was coming to terms with quickly. The glories of 1860 and 1861 were fading fast from the city's collective memory, and the victory that once seemed pre-determined now appeared hopelessly out of reach. Rhett might have seemed pessimistic to some, but Beauregard scarcely felt better about the Confederacy's prospects. His forts were battered, his men exhausted and outnumbered, and still the shelling continued. Perhaps that is why Beauregard did something he swore that he would never consider: He gave the fish-boat one more chance.

After the *Hunley* sank for a second time, locals began referring to it as the "peripatetic coffin" and similarly derisive names. Beauregard had ordered the sub to be scrapped, declaring that, "It is more dangerous to those who use it than the enemy." For that reason, the general might have ignored a request by Lt. George E. Dixon to refurbish the sub and raise another crew. But Beauregard had a problem. When Jefferson Davis visited Charleston, the general – eager to deliver any good news to the president – had let it slip that he had other methods of defending the harbor. He had to do something to back up that boast.

Dixon, who had fought under Beauregard at Shiloh, was a serious young man and he made a strong argument. He claimed the submarine was fully operational, that both of the previous accidents had been the result of operator error. He and his friend, the engineer William Alexander, had helped build the fish-boat in Mobile; they knew its capabilities and limitations. With a crew of their picking and enough time to train, Dixon and Alexander said, they could sink a blockade ship.

The work took weeks. Dixon and Alexander refurbished the submarine in Mount Pleasant and modified its method of attack. At Beauregard's insistence the *Hunley* was rigged with a spar exactly like those used on the *David*. During their work, a young artist named Conrad Wise Chapman stopped to sketch the fish-boat, a drawing that would inform perhaps his most famous painting. It showed the boat on blocks, the spar lying detached before it, hatches opened and nearly ready to sail again.

Dixon raised a new crew, mostly from the *Indian Chief*, and these men – old and young, American and immigrants among them – trained throughout December 1863 and January 1864. They stayed at a boarding house in Mount Pleasant and soon were testing the sub in the waters behind Sullivan's Island. Once, they had submerged to see how long they could remain underwater, and were down so long that the Confederates onshore reported that they had undoubtedly perished. Instead, they had passed their final test and were ready to attack the blockade.

If only the weather would cooperate. Dixon found himself grounded by the end of January, unable to brave the restless sea in such a delicate machine. He grew anxious, and a wound he had received at Shiloh must have bothered him constantly. During that battle, Dixon had been struck in the leg with a rifle ball; it hit a gold $20 piece in his pocket, driving the coin into his leg so deep it left a trench in his femur. But his life had been spared, and he had the coin engraved with the inscription "My life preserver."

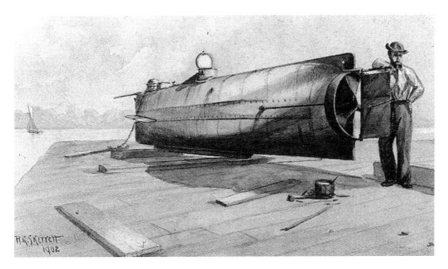

A sketch of the *H.L. Hunley.*

Dixon carried the coin with him as a good luck piece, but as the first month of 1864 ended he must have felt his luck had run out. In a letter to a friend, written in late January from his Mount Pleasant boarding house, Dixon lamented the great pressure placed on him by the Confederate military. The *Hunley* had to succeed; nothing less than Charleston itself was at stake.

"There is one thing very evident and that is to catch the Atlantic Ocean smooth during the winter months is considerable of an undertaking, and one that I never want to undertake again," Dixon wrote. "Especially when all parties interested are sitting at home and wondering and criticizing all of my actions and saying why don't he do something."

More than two weeks would pass before the weather calmed enough to provide Dixon with that chance. By then he had suffered a serious blow: Alexander had been called back to Mobile, where he was needed for his engineering genius. Dixon was forced to find a last-minute replacement, promote another man to be his first officer, and find a way to sink a blockade ship. His opportunity came on Feb. 17, 1864.

Around 6:30 that evening, the fish-boat pushed away from a dock on the north end of Sullivan's. It skirted the island's northern shore, passing through an inlet that separated Long Island from Sullivan's. And then the *Hunley* headed out to sea. It was not a fast boat. Running with the tide, which it was that night, it never exceeded 5

The USS *Housatonic*

mph. At that rate, it took more than two hours for the sub to reach its target.

Dixon guided the *Hunley* toward the USS *Housatonic,* a 205-foot sloop-of-war that ran on steam and sail power. It had been part of the blockade fleet for nearly a year and a half, but was not one of the more menacing Navy warships. The choice was based on geography more than anything else: the *Housatonic* was at the extreme northern end of the line of ships blocking the harbor. Help was a good ways off.

Dixon had promised Beauregard the *Hunley* would not attempt to submerge, even though his crew had trained for it. It was a promise Dixon was prepared to break if the need arose. But that night the sub traveled on the surface, cutting a slight wake through relatively calm seas. As it closed on the ship, a *Housatonic* sailor on bow watch spotted the boat. Rumors of the fish-boat had reached the blockading squadron and all the captains had been told to watch out for this danger beneath the waves. But the bow watch man, a free black sailor named Robert Flemming, could not get anyone to listen to his warnings. The officer on deck's refusal to listen would cost several men their lives.

By the time the *Housatonic's* officer recognized the threat, the *Hunley* was too close to turn a cannon on it. The sailors on deck fired rifles at the boat, aiming for a glowing light coming from the forward conning tower. Most bullets seemed to bounce off the sub's iron skin.

The *Hunley* rammed the *Housatonic*'s rear quarter with enough force to bury the barbed end of an explosive torpedo canister on the end of its spar deep into the warship's hull. Then the crew reversed the propeller, cranking backward to slip away from the *Housatonic*. As the sub retreated, the triggering line attached to the torpedo spun off its spool until finally it grew taut. And then, the entire flank of the ship disappeared in a single fiery explosion when 90 pounds of gunpowder was ignited.

The blast killed five men aboard the *Housatonic,* and it took only five minutes for the ship to sink. It came to rest on the shallow bottom, a bit of luck that allowed most of the crew to avoid drowning and hypothermia. They simply climbed into the ship's intricate rigging and waited for rescue. One of those sailors – Robert Flemming, the man who had first spotted the *Hunley* – said that about an hour after the attack, he saw something strange. Just ahead of the *Canandaigua,* the blockade ship coming to rescue them, Flemming thought he saw a light on the water. It looked almost blue.

The Confederates on Sullivan's Island saw the light, too, and later claimed it was a signal from Dixon. The sub captain had told the men that when they saw his beacon they should start a signal fire on the beach so he could find his way back to Sullivan's. Troops lit a bonfire that night, but they would never know if Dixon saw it. Shortly after the attack, Dixon, his crew and the *Hunley* disappeared, taking Charleston's last hope to breaking the blockade with them.

St. Michael's Church, 1865

CHAPTER 19

'A FUTURE MOST AWFUL'

T he Confederate flag was falling. It tumbled slow-motion through the smoke toward the rubble below with only its white field visible in the haze. At that moment it looked very much like a flag of surrender.

Lt. C.H. Claiborne saw the shell hit the flagstaff, snapping the pole in two – a lucky shot, and only the second of the day from the Yankees. On June 20, 1864, it appeared the Stainless Banner would be just another casualty in the ongoing bombardment of Fort Sumter, another fallen soldier. But Claiborne could not allow that to happen. The flag of the Confederacy must not touch the ground.

He was the only one who could make it in time. Sgt. Shaffer was closer but he was down, hit by the splintered flagstaff. So the lieutenant ran across the parapet, dodging shrapnel and inhaling smoke the whole way, with a single thought in his mind: He would not let the Yankees see how good their aim had been. The Confederate flag might fall one day, but not on this one.

He reached the flag just in time, catching it in mid-air a second before it landed on the parapet. By the time the smoke cleared, Claiborne was holding the flag defiantly above his head. Two engineers – N.F. Devareaux and B. Brannon – saw what had happened and rushed to Claiborne's aid. As he stood there in the line of fire, the two men worked to replant the flagstaff. Soon, Union gunners spotted the trio and opened fire, "too cowardly to appreciate, and too mean to honor a gallant act in a foe," the *Mercury* would later note.

The three soldiers ignored the assault and eventually re-hoisted the flag high over the battered fort. Before they ducked back into the relative safety of Sumter's crumbling walls, Claiborne, Devareaux and Brannon "saluted the enemy with a cheer and a wave of their hats." It was a patriotic display of defiance, one the *Mercury* would call "one of the most heroic acts of bravery connected with the history of the bombardment of Fort Sumter."

Robert Barnwell Rhett Jr. gave the story prominent space in the pages of his newspaper a week after the event. It was a minor incident, but Rhett played it up because Charleston was desperate for uplifting news by the summer of 1864. It had been a demoralizing spring. More than 2,000 shots had been fired against Sumter, further reducing the might – and profile – of the city's flagship fort. At the same time, the bombardment of the city had continued on and off, the Confederates offering less resistance than locals would have liked.

Good news was in short supply all around. Through March the *Hunley*'s successful attack on the USS *Housatonic* filled the newspaper's pages, most accounts reprinted from Northern newspapers. It was the best news Charleston had had in months, made better by Yankee editors fretting about the possibility that the South had six or eight of these infernal stealth boats. The *Mercury* did little to dissuade such speculation. Although Rhett never named the boat responsible for the attack, he abetted the Confederate cause by suggesting that it was still on the prowl.

"We are glad to be able to assure our readers that the boat and crew are now safe," the *Mercury* reported.

In truth, the *Hunley* was lost and no one in Charleston knew what had happened to it. The Confederates did not even know its attack had succeeded until 10 days later when Southerners captured a Union picket boat and the captured sailors reported the news. The men said as a result of the torpedo boat's assault "all the wooden vessels of the blockading squadron now go far out to sea every night, being afraid of the risk of riding at anchor in any portion of the outer harbor."

To maintain the charade, Beauregard dispatched the *David* on two attacks that spring. In early March, the torpedo boat engaged the USS *Memphis* in the North Edisto River. The little boat struck the *Memphis* twice, its torpedo reportedly failing to explode each time. In April the *David* tried to sink a blockade ship, the USS *Wabash*. The Union crew spotted the ship and was able to avoid being hit, but was unable to sink the *David*.

Between those two attacks, Charleston suffered another serious setback. On March 19 a fire broke out in the Confederate States Arsenal. One simple spark set off 20 pounds of powder in the arsenal's "pyrotechnic room," a wooden building at the Ashley Avenue complex. Several soldiers were injured, and one man, Emanuel Hogan, succumbed to smoke inhalation during the blaze. He was unable to escape in time because of a prior injury: Hogan had lost a leg a year earlier at the Battle of Battery Wagner.

The *Mercury* noted that the accident, while horrible, could have been worse. It was as much optimism as Rhett could muster. The Confederacy was quickly coming to grips with the possibility of defeat. Every week brought another editorial concerned with the uncertain future facing the South: "What Remains of the War" followed by "The Vindications of History." From Richmond, Confederate President Jefferson Davis declared April 8 a day of fasting and prayer, which only served as another excuse for Rhett to contemplate the South's fate.

"We are on the eve of events big with the destiny of ourselves and our posterity," Rhett wrote. "A future the most awful that the imagination can contemplate awaits us if we fail; a future glorious and happy if we succeed."

Beauregard tried to raise the local morale by hosting a ceremony reminiscent of those held so frequently in the early days of the war. On April 13 the Confederates marked the anniversary of their capture of Fort Sumter with a 13-gun salute. It did not go smoothly. An hour before the program started, a Yankee Parrott shell hit the fort, killing Pvt. Joseph P. Huger. And as the Southerners fired their ceremonial shells, the Union guns on Morris Island hurled 20 mortars into the city.

By the spring of 1864 Charleston bore little resemblance to its grand, antebellum self. Its central business district gutted by fire, the homes of the lower peninsula deserted, the city had become little more than an outpost for soldiers. The Charleston of old barely existed, the troops left to defend a ghost of a town. Most days there was little news to report – another fire, a ship that managed to get past the blockade and into the city. On a good day, no shells were hurled at Charleston. On a bad one, lives were lost.

In April one shot hit Mr. Duncan's blacksmith shop on Hasell Street. The shell crashed through the roof and landed on an anvil where a young slave boy named

Aaron was working. Doctors later reported that the boy's left arm would have to be amputated, but he would likely survive. Weeks later another shell shattered another child's arm. He too lived. As a result of this onslaught of artillery and bad news, the entire city's nerves were frayed.

The *Mercury* was forced to devote an increasing amount of its columns to crime news. On Friday, March 18, officer McSweeney of the Charleston Police Department arrested a Pvt. Young of the 1st S.C. Infantry for some unrecorded offense. Young, however, drew his pistol and shot McSweeney, "the ball entering his abdomen, and coming out at the back." Young was eventually jailed. McSweeney, the newspaper reported, was doing well and "it is hoped he will recover."

Just after daybreak on Saturday, May 7, a police officer on patrol found a runaway slave named Christopher lying at the corner of Beaufain and Rutledge, a gunshot wound to his abdomen. The 18-year-old — owned by Hugh E. Vincent, the paper noted — had been missing for a year and a half, and claimed that he had been robbed and shot by soldiers. The slave was taken first to the guard house and then to the hospital, but by then it was too late. He died around noon.

The newspaper was not averse to reporting crimes allegedly committed by soldiers, but Rhett raised questions about the accuracy of Christopher's story, which he carried to his death bed. The residence of J.C.E. Richardson on Rutledge, not far from the corner where the young slave was found, had been robbed. Richardson was out of town, like so many Charleston residents, but had left his home booby-trapped.

There was really only one window in the house suitable for thieves, and Richardson had set up his gun with a double-shot of ball and buckshot pointed at the window. If the shutter was opened, the gun would go off. The *Mercury* reported that the gun had been fired, and surmised that Christopher had been shot while trying to rob Richardson's house. Whether that was what happened, it sounded better than the alternative, that the South's own soldiers were killing people in the streets of Charleston.

In the early days of the war, the *Mercury* printed almost exclusively positive news items about events around town. As the summer of 1864 approached, however, stories of women delivering clothes to the crew of the CSS *Indian Chief* were the exception. Instead the paper devoted ample space to denouncing rumors such as the one circulating on May 18 that said Richmond had fallen. Someone claimed that blockade ships had fired guns that day in salute to Union troops taking the Confederate capital. The fact that the rumor was false provided little comfort to a city under siege.

On Sunday, May 22, the North began yet another concerted push to take James Island. Union ships sailed into the Stono River and began to bombard Secessionville. At the same time, between 800 and 1,000 Yankees attempted to come ashore at Le-

View of Meeting Street, looking south toward the Circular Church, the Mills House, and St. Michael's Church.

gare's Farm. They were repelled by local troops, but soon they would once again have a foothold on the island. It was the beginning of the summer's escalation.

By July 2 an estimated 1,500 Northern troops descended on James Island, where they fell into a brutal fight with Confederate forces. It seemed that this exercise, largely unsuccessful, was meant to distract the South from a much larger assault on Fort Johnson. The next day, a Sunday, 48 barges filled with Yankee troops approached the James Island fort. Lt. Col. Joseph A. Yates trained all his guns on the barges, which sent the enemy boats scurrying for cover. Only 11 of the barges were noticed returning to Battery Gregg on Morris Island. Yates confirmed that at least five boats were captured in the attack, netting Fort Johnson 140 prisoners.

That same weekend Union Brig. Gen. John P. Hatch landed on Seabrook Island with 4,000 troops, planning to cross Johns Island and destroy the bridges to Charleston. The troops made it onto Johns Island but the intense Lowcountry heat slowed their march to a crawl, so much so that it took days to reach the Stono side of the island. Their delay doomed the mission. One regiment and an artillery battery charged Confederate troops at Waterloo plantation but met with heavy fire and were forced to retreat quickly.

The next day Battery Pringle on James Island opened fire on the Yankees, which didn't result in any casualties but rattled the Union soldiers. Finally, on July 9, Col. George P. Harrison Jr. led Georgia troops against the federal line, a bloody battle that saw at least 100 casualties. When some of the federal troops managed to outflank the Confederate troops, they soon met 21 men from Capt. Tillman H. Clark's Second South Carolina Cavalry. Out of that small group, seven men were killed, another six injured. But somehow they managed to stop a much larger Union force. The battle of Bloody Bridge was over.

For the rest of the month, the two sides engaged in a number of minor skirmishes across James and Johns islands. Most were stalemates. The Union held its ground at the edge of the islands, but could not advance – a testament to the resolve of Southern forces, which were stretched thin at that moment. On July 7 the third major assault of Fort Sumter had begun. It was the most punishing offensive in more than a year, and the South needed every man available to defend it.

The bombardment would continue for more than two months. Most days, more than 100 shells hit Sumter, and on some as many as 350 shots rained down on the decimated fort. The average was more than 200 shots per day, and the shelling was doing its share of damage. On July 20, Capt. John C. Mitchell, the commander at Fort Sumter, was killed in the bombing. A week later, an engineer named John Johnson was hit by a mortar round and died instantly.

Fort Sumter would bring in a new commander, Capt. Thomas Huguenin of the 1st S.C. Regular Infantry, and other soldiers would rise up to fill the positions of their fallen comrades. It was a never-ending cycle as the summer of 1864 dragged on. Between July 7 and Sept. 4, Union guns would hurl 14,600 shells at Sumter, killing 81 Confederates. After a day's respite, the guns re-opened on the fort for another 12 days. In that time, nearly 600 more shells would be fired at the fort, killing another half-dozen men.

But by then, it was almost over.

In September, Atlanta fell.

The battle had consumed much of the summer, stretching north from the city all the way to Chattanooga, Tenn. Ultimately, Maj. Gen. William T. Sherman managed to get the best of the Southern troops. When Sherman cut off the Confederates' supply line, Lt. Gen. John Bell Hood had little recourse but to evacuate Atlanta on Sept. 1, burning supply depots and ammunition to keep them from falling into enemy hands. The next day, Atlanta's mayor presented his city to Sherman.

Charleston residents were devastated by the news. The *Mercury* followed Hood's retreat and printed news of the Union's movements from Georgia newspapers almost daily, but Rhett refrained from speculating on what this meant for the Holy City. He didn't need to say anything; most people realized the South was in trouble. It took yet another local disaster to distract Charleston residents from the plight of Atlanta.

On Saturday, Sept. 17 a two-story building on Clifford Street caught fire in the middle of the day. Four small buildings on the street and the lecture room at the German Lutheran Church were destroyed. Sparks from the flames ignited a house on Beresford Street and the fire began to spread. Ten buildings on Archdale Street eventually burned, including the hall of the German Friendly Society, a tenement building and the home of a free black woman. Before firemen extinguished the blaze, it had traveled all the way from Beaufain Street to Tradd and Meeting streets.

"The city has been visited by a conflagration more extensive and serious in its character than any that has occurred since the memorable disaster of '61," the *Mercury* reported.

Between this latest fire and the continued shelling, locals could hardly help but notice that Charleston was looking more like Atlanta every day.

The next week Charleston residents were crestfallen to learn that Beauregard – who had been out of the city since April – would not return. The *Mercury* reported various rumors about the general's new orders. In a front-page editorial, Rhett speculated that "(t)he President has gone to the army in Georgia to endeavor to arrange matters, without putting General Beauregard in command – that is, to reconcile, if possible, the army to General Hood's continuation in its command. If he succeeds, according to his estimation, General Beauregard will be returned to his command near Petersburg. If he fails, General Beauregard will be ordered to the command of the army in Georgia."

Beauregard's ultimate destination mattered less than the fact that he was gone. The man who had led Charleston's resistance and fended off the Yankees for the better part of the war was no longer the city's defender. When the general and his staff arrived on Sept. 25 for a brief layover en route to his new assignment, it was a bittersweet visit for locals. He left for Augusta on Oct. 1, saying goodbye to Confederate Charleston for the last time.

October was a brutal month in the city. On the night following Beauregard's departure, Battery Gregg fired 32 shots into the city. A few days of shelling would be followed by a day or two of eerie quiet. The weekend of Oct. 15 was particularly violent as Union guns lobbed 134 shells at the city. For those souls who remained in Charleston, the bombardment was becoming a normal occurrence – that is, as close to normal as was possible for a city that had been under siege for more than a year.

The month ended with a disturbing scene on the peninsula. On Oct. 25 one shell hit "in the more exposed portion of the city," the *Mercury* recounted, and hit a house occupied by several Confederate troops. Pvt. John Shannon was killed in the explosion, while Lieutenants L.P. Mays, John Dardon and D.E. Willis were gravely injured. Mays and Dardon were wounded so badly they would not survive amputation surgeries. Only Willis escaped with his life. The casualties were mounting, and the *Mercury* could do little but tally the war dead and report on the ever-increasing instances of crime committed on the peninsula.

Gen. William T. Sherman inspects battlements in Atlanta prior to his "march to the sea." After his capture of Atlanta, Sherman went on to capture Savannah and divide the Confederate States of America.

On Nov. 10, the 490th day of the siege, the *Mercury* grudgingly reported that the quick succession of cannon fire heard coming from Morris Island the prior Tuesday had actually marked the end of a party. Rhett noted with no small amount of distaste that the "grand frolic" was occasioned by soldiers and free blacks celebrating their "intelligent votes in favor of the permanence of the Lincoln dynasty."

"About dark the shouting and cheering of the enemy could be distinctly heard over the quiet waters of the harbor," Rhett wrote. "In point of fact the mongrel Morris Islanders are believed to have been all gloriously drunk."

As the fall of 1864 settled in the Yankees were the only ones around Charleston with cause to celebrate. Beauregard was gone, the city suffered from regular shelling and a seemingly endless series of crimes and fires. But that was not the worst of it. By December many city residents were most concerned by the rumors starting to come out of Georgia.

Sherman was marching to the sea.

Houses on the Battery damaged by shell fire.

CHAPTER 20

CITY OF RUIN

C harleston was quiet on the 514th day of the siege.

The Confederate and Union troops had agreed to a temporary truce to exchange prisoners, a bureaucratic ordeal that the *Mercury* predicted would take "two weeks or thereabouts" to complete. Under this arrangement the shelling of the city was suspended, allowing weary residents a welcome chance to relax. But it would not last. On this day – Monday, Dec. 5, 1864 – someone would not get the message in time.

For reasons that were never clear, the terms of the truce had not been fully communicated to the staff at Fort Sumter. A sharpshooter at his post that day spotted a Union soldier at Battery Gregg in plain sight, making no effort to hide. The Southerner watched the Yankee for a moment, then steadied his gun, took aim and fired. The man fell immediately – wounded or killed, the newspaper did not know – and the ceasefire was over.

Battery Gregg opened its guns on the fort at once, the shots echoing through the city. Soon other Union batteries on Morris Island joined in the shelling and the mortars rained down on Sumter mercilessly for several minutes. Finally, the fort's officers raised a white flag and the shooting slowly wound down. The Southerners sent a note of apology to Battery Gregg, explained the mistake and the uneasy truce resumed.

The entire city was on edge as winter came to the Lowcountry. Each day brought new reports of Sherman's march to the sea. The despised Union general was making his way southeast through Georgia to Savannah – on that day he was a mere 60 miles from the port – and there was little doubt he would soon capture the city. It seemed no one could stop the man who had taken Atlanta, and Charleston residents worried that they would soon be in the general's sights.

On Dec. 12 the *Mercury* reported that the Savannah Railroad's tracks had been "menaced" by Yankee shelling, cutting off Charleston's rail access to the south. A week later, on Dec. 20, Sherman and his men reached the Savannah River and within two days Rhett reported that Confederate troops had abandoned the Georgia city. The next morning, Savannah's mayor rode out to greet the general. Hoping to avoid the fate of Atlanta, he offered to surrender in exchange for Sherman's promise to protect the city's property and residents.

Savannah was under Yankee rule by the day's end.

Sherman offered the city to President Lincoln as a Christmas present, but most Charleston residents feared the gift that Lincoln wanted most lay 100 miles up the coast. By Christmas 1864, however, Charleston was not much of a prize. The city was in ruins, more a victim of fire than the shells that pounded the peninsula each week. The mail service was spotty and many residents had fled months before. Those who remained were subjected to an ever-increasing number and variety of crimes.

On New Year's Eve the *Mercury* recounted numerous outrages that had plagued the city during the final week of 1864. Someone had fired five or six shots into a house on Bull Street; a man was mugged on Coming Street, beaten and robbed of $1,200; a free black man was knocked down on Cannon Street, stripped of his coat and $100. And then, the younger brother of the local provost marshal was assaulted by three soldiers who demanded money and "something to drink."

But perhaps the most disturbing incident came on Dec. 29. Around 9 on that Thursday evening, a group of soldiers tried to force their way into a "respectable home" on Smith Street. There were five or six of them and they made so much noise they attracted the neighbors' attention. A woman who lived across the street saw what was happening and called out to a servant in the house, asking if "the colonel" was home to protect them.

The slave replied the "master was absent on duty" and that there was no one in the house except servants and several young women. Still, the soldiers could not get inside. Ultimately they grew so frustrated that one of the men fired a shot through a first-floor window. The ball hit a wall and rebounded, falling at the feet of one of the young ladies. It was most miraculous, the *Mercury* said, that no one was injured.

War or no, Charleston had become a very dangerous place.

The Great Fire of 1861 destroyed many of Charleston's most famous landmarks, including the Circular Church (left) and Institute Hall. St. Philips Church, seen in the distance, was spared.

On Jan. 4, 1865 the *Mercury* reported that more than 100,000 Confederate soldiers were absent without leave. In a front-page editorial, Rhett blamed the Southern government. He reminded his readers that "(h)istory tells of no struggles for independence in which more general and heroic devotion was ever displayed." He wrote that intermeddling, prejudices and petty partisanship "weigh like a pall upon the heart of the country" and were destroying the Confederacy. The country needed its men, many more than could be gained from prisoner exchanges. And they needed them quickly. On that same day, the paper reported that Sherman had crossed into South Carolina and was near Hardeeville — barely 80 miles south of the city.

"All the beef cattle, hogs and sheep have been driven from the Hardeeville and Grahamville sections, and are now pastured in a safe locality," the paper noted.

Sherman's men were making fine progress of their own accord; no one in the state wanted to help their march by providing them with dinner.

As 1865 dawned on Charleston, the remaining residents had to contend with both the possibility of invasion and the rising crime rate. By then it seemed that Southerners were menacing the city as much, if not more, than the Yankees. After a house at the corner of Coming and Wentworth streets was robbed of more than $3,000 in supplies, locals began to speculate that a group of men masquerading as Confederate soldiers were behind the rash of robbings, muggings and thefts.

"The fact that a few prowling stragglers in the garb of soldiers have been unwarrantably assuming the functions of a provost guard, stopping and robbing negroes, and in some cases, white men, has thrown discredit upon many of patrols of the bona fide provost guard," the newspaper reported. "In order therefore to prevent mistakes, we would mention that there is a genuine provost guard, relief parties from which perform the onerous duty of patrolling the streets at all hours, night and day, and the best plan for citizens and others, when challenged, will be to show their papers without delay."

As if all this weren't enough, Battery Gregg resumed the shelling of Fort Sumter at 3 a.m. on Sunday, Jan. 8. But it seemed like the Union Army was just going through the motions. The Yankees had fired about 44,000 rounds at the fort in a year's time. At this point, there was hardly anything left standing.

Disheartening as the city's predicament had become, the fight had not gone out of Charleston completely. Rhett soon launched into a vicious verbal assault on Confederate officials in Richmond who were rumored to be considering a peace accord with the North — a treaty that might include limitations on the expansion of slavery. On the front page of the *Mercury*, the editor called this "lunacy" and predicted that South Carolina would fight to the bitter end.

"It was on account of encroachments upon the institution of slavery by the sectional majority of the old Union, that South Carolina seceded from that Union," Rhett wrote. "It is not at this late day, after the loss of thirty thousand of her best and bravest men in battle, that she will suffer it to be bartered away; or ground between the upper and nether mill stones, by the madness of Congress, or the counsels of shallow men elsewhere. ... We want no Confederate government without our institutions. And we will have none."

South Carolina, Rhett declared, would not abandon its principles, "Sink or swim, live or die" — and with or without Virginia and the Confederate Congress.

Charleston residents got a glimpse of Rhett's predicted "future of subjugation" when the *Mercury* published a report out of Savannah on Jan. 14. Every man, woman and child in the Georgia city had been ordered to take an oath, the newspaper said, "not simply of neutrality, not a parol not to fight against the United States, but an oath of allegiance, not alone to the Constitution of the United States, but to the unconstitutional laws which have been passed by an abolition Congress."

Charleston's spirits were so low that not even the destruction of a hated blockade ship warranted much excitement. On Sunday night, Jan. 15, the men at Fort Sumter had watched a Union ironclad drift into and out of sight in a heavy fog. The troops estimated it was about 600 yards off, and they were waiting for the boat to get a little closer before they opened fire.

Aboard the USS *Patapsco*, the crew was providing cover for two Union picket boats dragging the harbor entrance for mines. The Confederates could not see the small picket boats, only the ironclad's rounded turret. The fog left the *Patapsco* as blind as the sentries at Sumter, and some of the crew was on deck taking constant soundings to make sure the boat didn't run aground. And then, about 8 p.m., the ironclad found one of those submerged Confederate mines – when it hit the ship's hull.

The explosion was muffled by the water enough that the men at Sumter did not hear it. Even the crew of the *Patapsco* did not realize at first how seriously their vessel had been damaged. But within a minute, the heavy, cumbersome boat began to sink into the channel. Some crew members managed to get away, but more than 60 Union sailors went down with the ship. The sentries at Sumter would later report that they suddenly heard "a confused mingling of shouts ... and cries for mercy" that quickly died away.

It was a hollow victory for the South. Their mines had protected the harbor, but everyone in Charleston had to wonder for how much longer?

By the end of January, Sherman was rumored to be on the move.

The *Mercury* reported that the general's troops had advanced to Branchville "with a considerable force of infantry." The Yankees had not made more progress, Rhett speculated, because of poor road conditions. Other reports claimed Union troops were planning an attack on the railroad. At the same time more U.S. forces were crossing the Savannah River and into the state at Sister's Ferry. It appeared the endgame was near. But for the moment Charleston was quiet.

There was so little news in the city that Rhett granted front-page space to the rants of a man who had recently arrived in town to give Charleston news of the coming peace. "This 'reliable gentleman,'" as the *Mercury* derisively called him, "has now taken up lodgings in Charleston, and can be seen any day upon the street with his mouth wide open, and his tongue going like the clapper of a town bell. Yesterday his oracles were a little more cheerful than the day before. To amuse our readers, we will give his last on the 'Peace Commission.'"

According to Rhett, the man claimed Lincoln had offered reunion with slavery preserved on the same basis as before the war — so long as fugitive slaves did not have to be returned and that there would be no expansion of slavery to the territories. But Confederate President Jefferson Davis had rejected these terms and all of Lincoln's other overtures. Despite the *Mercury*'s prominent reporting on the "reliable gentleman" and his claims, Rhett called it crazy talk.

"The situation is simple, and our destiny is plain — the Yankees must be driven from the soil of the Confederation, or the people of the Confederate States must be driven from their own soil — white slavery and expatriotism or independence and black slavery," Rhett wrote. "Let all men hush with the foolish talk of peace, and let there be but one watchword, from one end of the land to the other — Fight!"

Charleston residents, isolated from the rest of the South, found it difficult to sort through all the conflicting, contradictory rumors. By the second week of February 1865 they began to hear stories that the war would soon end. This news was distressing enough, but then a more ominous rumor surfaced: The Confederate military was making plans to abandon the city. The *Mercury* – the newspaper which had promoted secession and the war so fiercely – seemed unwilling to face any such prospects. Rhett, at least, did not want to give up.

All that would change within a few days.

On Friday morning, Feb. 10, federal barges escorted by Union gunboats landed between 3,000 and 4,000 Union troops on James Island at Grimball's plantation. The soldiers pushed Confederate pickets back to their nearest defenses, but beyond that the fight was a stalemate. Maj. Edward Manigault of the Palmetto Battalion was reportedly killed in the skirmish, "but some doubt is expressed as to the correctness of this report." In fact, Manigault was wounded and taken prisoner. The last report of the day said the U.S. forces were slowly advancing, while simultaneously other Union troops had attacked the line at Salkehatchie and a third group was moving up the Charleston road. Sherman had crossed the Edisto, but suddenly it appeared he had turned his attention toward Augusta. It mattered little which troops came. The fact remained that Northern forces were descending on the city.

The same day this alarming news was delivered Rhett announced that the *Mercury* would cease publication – at least temporarily. In a note "To our Readers," Rhett wrote that "the interruption of railroad communication between Charleston and the interior produces a state of affairs that compels us, temporarily, to transfer the publication office of the *Mercury* elsewhere; and today's paper will be our last issue, for the present, in the city of Charleston."

He said the newspaper would shut down only for a few days, but the *Mercury* would not publish again for 21 months. By then Charleston had changed irrevocably.

That weekend, the Morris Island batteries turned on the city once more, their new guns so effective that some shells landed north of Calhoun Street. It seemed that no corner of the city was safe any longer. Many of the remaining residents, believing rumors of an imminent troop withdrawal, fled the city to the South Carolina interior. It was apparent that Charleston was quickly becoming a lost cause.

Perhaps it was fitting that the orders, when they came, were dispatched by Gen. Beauregard. On Feb. 14, he sent word for the Confederate military to abandon Charleston. The general had believed Sherman was headed for the city up until a few days before that, but soon he realized it didn't matter. The South could no longer hold the city where secession and the war began.

It took a few days to make all the preparations and in that time Union signalmen managed to figure out what was going on. The Confederates were reducing their rations stock, moving hospitals farther inland and inspecting wagon trains for brigades that had not moved during the war. Yankee spotters deciphered one message sent to Sullivan's Island that read, "Burn all papers before you leave."

The Confederate troops put on a show until the end. On the morning of Feb. 17, they raised a new Confederate flag over Fort Sumter. When they lowered the banner that evening, the soldiers followed it out, abandoning Sumter in the dead of night. Fort Moultrie and Castle Pinckney would follow suit, leaving their colors flying to keep the Yankees at bay for as long as possible.

It was, historian Milby Burton would later write, a night of "horror and chaos, undoubtedly the worst ever experienced in the history of the city." Fire, which had caused so much distress to Charleston during the war, would usher out the Confederacy. In public squares soldiers burned piles of cotton and rice to keep the supplies from Union soldiers. The troops tried to set fire to the Arsenal in order to deprive the Yankees of Southern ammunition, but weren't able to ignite the stock. They fared better with their other attempts at sabotage. The magazine at Battery Bee on Sullivan's Island was blown up, shaking the entire island. Troops burned the bridge over the Ashley River, and set off a charge that took out a huge Blakely gun on The Battery.

The Confederates saved 20 tons of powder for the gunboats. The *Chicora* and the *Charleston* were blown up, pieces of the *Charleston* raining down on the city wharves. Finally, the soldiers turned to the Ladies' Gunboat. The *Palmetto State* was burned to the waterline – a symbolic sacrifice that said, as much as anything, that Charleston was resigned to its fate. Later, some people would claim that, in the smoke rising out of the sinking gunboat, they saw the image of a palmetto tree.

Most of the fires were allowed to burn through the night. Many of the city's firefighters had fled, leaving only a couple of companies composed of free blacks to fight the blazes. Bands of looters ran through the streets and the people who didn't evacuate the city barricaded themselves in their homes. The horrors of war had come to their front doors.

It was the 585th day of the Siege of Charleston and by morning it would be over.

The blockading fleet had heard the explosions and realized that something was happening in Charleston. A few ships soon crept toward the harbor, wary of a trap. Union soldiers at one of the Morris Island batteries spotted a group of Confederate pickets fleeing Sullivan's Island, apparently headed for the bridge to Mount Pleasant.

The Yankee guns opened fire but the Southerners managed to escape.

The turreted-ironclad *Canonicus* was the first gunboat to approach the harbor. The crew spied the Confederate flag flying over Fort Moultrie but thought the outpost looked deserted. They decided to test their suspicion by firing two shots into the fort. When Moultrie did not respond, word spread quickly. The Southerners had retreated. Those two shots fired by the *Canonicus* were the last hurled at Charleston in the Civil War.

The Yankees soon landed at Fort Sumter and hoisted the regimental flag of the 52nd Pennsylvania, the first U.S. flag to fly over the fort since 1861. After years of fighting and nearly 50,000 rounds fired at the fort, the Union was able to take Sumter only because the Confederates had ceded it. But by then, Fort Sumter bore little resemblance to the outpost it had once been. Entire walls had been reduced to rubble, the remains of which were scattered across the man-made island. In that respect, it matched the rest of the city it had defended for nearly four years.

Once the word spread, blockade ships steamed into Charleston Harbor. A few raced to be the first boat to raise the U.S. flag over Castle Pinckney. Lt. Col. Augustus Bennett and the 21st U.S. Colored Troops landed at Mills Wharf at the foot of Broad Street, near the Exchange Building, around 10 that morning. They found the city smoking and eerily quiet. Looters had broken out windows across the city, stealing what few valuables remained in storefronts. It appeared the city had been ransacked and then deserted.

Bennett and Hennessy were met by city alderman George W. Williams, who carried a letter from Mayor Charles Macbeth that surrendered Charleston. Williams told them the Confederate military had abandoned the city overnight and that local officials had remained behind to try and save it. But the task was too much for them. He asked if Union troops might arrest the looters and extinguish the fires.

There was no one else left in Charleston to do it.

The Fifty-fifth Massachusetts Colored Regiment singing John Brown's March in the streets of Charleston, February 21, 1865.

THE CAUSE, LOST

W illiam Tecumseh Sherman captured the South Carolina capital on the day Confederate troops were making their final preparations to leave Charleston. The fires that destroyed Columbia in his wake would remain controversial for more than a century: Did Gen. Wade Hampton's retreating Confederates set the fires to destroy supplies, were they accidental, or did Sherman's men burn the city? It would only fuel the controversy later, when a letter from the general revealed that U.S. troops were itching to punish the state that had started this war.

"The truth is the whole army is burning with an insatiable desire to wreak vengeance upon South Carolina," Sherman wrote to Washington officials. "I almost tremble at her fate."

The fate of Charleston was no less severe. The city was not burned by occupying Union forces, but then there was no need. Very little of Charleston was left untouched by either the fire of 1861 or those set by the retreating Confederates. Looters and vandals did the rest. The Union sent soldiers from the 21st U.S. Colored Troops to take possession of the city and restore order in the days after the Southern military abandoned it. But some locals later claimed the soldiers, rather than stopping the looting, paraded through the streets and joined the melee.

By the end of February citizens of Charleston were ordered to take an oath of allegiance to the United States, not unlike the one residents of Savannah had been forced to accept months earlier. Those few souls who had not escaped the city lived in fear of the Yankees for months. A New York regiment arrived to augment the 21st and eventually the U.S. Army would order its troops to return all items taken from Charleston homes. But for a while there was no appreciable difference. As late as March soldiers reported that some troops were breaking into homes near Magnolia Cemetery, taking whatever they could carry, the occupants powerless to stop them.

Eventually, Sherman himself visited Charleston to see the destruction firsthand. He was somewhat familiar with the city; he had been stationed at Fort Moultrie early in his career. But what he saw resembled nothing more than a skeleton of the grand antebellum city he had known. The man so despised in Charleston was nonetheless saddened by the city's pitiful condition.

"Any one who is not satisfied with war should go and see Charleston," Sherman later wrote, "and he will pray louder and deeper than ever that the country may in the long future be spared any more war."

The fall of Charleston attracted several Northern journalists who were eager for a glimpse of the birthplace of war. These reporters recorded the city's activities in the days after Robert Barnwell Rhett Jr. abandoned it. Charles Carleton Coffin, a writer with the Boston *Journal*, was one of the first to arrive. He had been aboard one of the blockade ships that steamed into the harbor in February, and his account painted a sad portrait of desolation, destruction and a cause that had been lost. He called Charleston, "A city of ruins – silent, mournful, in deepest humiliation."

Coffin explored the city for several days, describing the aftermath of the siege to Northern audiences. The Swamp Angel battery had beaten him to the offices of the *Mercury*, he wrote. A shell had hit the newspaper office's roof, exploded in the chimney and sent bricks raining down on the editorial room. The Mills House on Meeting Street sat with boarded up windows, and the Charleston Hotel, farther north on the same street, had several gaping holes in it – further evidence of the range of the Union guns.

At St. Michael's Episcopal Church, perhaps the most recognizable building in the city, pews were in splinters and the windows were shattered, glass lying in the streets. Bombs had torn through St. Philip's as well. The church looked as if it had been abandoned long ago, its yard a ratty collection of weeds. Somewhere on those grounds, Southerners had hidden the body of John C. Calhoun, fearing Yankees would deface his grave. It would lay hidden through most of Reconstruction.

Late in his tour, Coffin stumbled upon a scene that would haunt him for the rest of his life. On Chalmers Street he found a building with a large iron gate across its entrance, the word "MART" affixed to the wrought iron in gilt letters. It was the remains of what perhaps had been the city's largest slave market. Peering through that gate Coffin saw a hall about 60 feet long, "flanked on one side by a long table running the entire length of the hall, and on the other by benches." Beyond the hall, a locked door led into a yard that held another building. Coffin kicked at the door but it would not give. Eventually a black man came along and the two hoisted a large stone, beat it against the door and eventually broke through.

The centerpiece of the interior yard was a four-story brick building with grated windows and iron doors – "a prison," Coffin wrote. "He who entered there left all hope behind." Coffin saw a room where women "were subjected to the lascivious gaze of brutal men" and the stairs that led onto the stage, where thousands of human beings had been sold into bondage. As Coffin stood looking at the auction block, he heard a voice behind him.

"I was sold there upon that table two years ago."

Her name was Dinah More, Coffin would later write, and she was one of the thousands of enslaved Africans who had passed through that gate as property. She had come that day, the same as Coffin, out of curiosity. But perhaps she had felt the need to come back to the Mart for one final look at that stage, to know that it would never be used again. The reporter reassured her of that.

"You never will be sold again," Coffin told her. "You are free now and forever."

"Thank God," More said. "O the blessed Jesus, he has heard my prayer. I am so glad; only I wish I could see my husband. He was sold at the same time into the country, and has gone I don't know where."

Coffin was so touched by the scene he took several artifacts from the Slave Mart, reminders of the horrors he'd seen. He stole a gilt star off the front gate and took steps leading to the stage. He carried both back to Boston, relics of the lost cause.

In March Gen. Robert E. Lee and the Army of Northern Virginia engaged Gen. Grant's forces at Petersburg one final time. After months of trench warfare, the Confederates could not get the upper hand. Little more than a week later Richmond fell and the Southern cause was lost. On April 9, 1865, a few days shy of the war's fourth anniversary, Gen. Lee surrendered to Ulysses S. Grant at Appomattox Courthouse.

To pass the time that day, Army of the Potomac played the Army of Northern Virginia in an impromptu game of baseball. It was the first step in what would be a long process of healing and reunion. But it was a start.

Although some fighting would continue for weeks before word finally spread across the country, the Civil War was officially over. Confederate President Jefferson Davis was eventually arrested in Georgia, and some Northerners would claim he tried to evade capture by dressing as a woman (he had, Southerners maintained, mistakenly taken his wife's overcoat in the rush to escape). Davis would be imprisoned at Fort Monroe, Va. for two years on charges of treason. He was ultimately released on bail, supplied in part by Northern newspaper editors and railroad owner Cornelius Vanderbilt. The U.S. government eventually dropped the charges.

The Civil War remains the country's bloodiest conflict. More than 620,000 Americans died in four years of battles – more than all the United States' other wars combined. Fewer than half of those deaths were the result of actual combat; nearly as many were the result of disease or more pedestrian causes. Less than a week after Lee's surrender, there was one more casualty: President Abraham Lincoln was assassinated in Washington by Confederate sympathizer John Wilkes Booth.

Union forces would occupy Charleston for more than a decade during Reconstruction. The Charleston *Mercury* resumed publication on Monday, Nov. 19, 1866, with Robert Barnwell Rhett Jr. at the helm again. In its first editorial, the newspaper recounted the end of the war and tried to strike a tone that was alternately conciliatory and defiant in its epilogue to "40 years of effort."

"In referring to the Past, we have no desire to extenuate, to paliate, or to excuse the part that the *Mercury* has played in the politics of the country. We do not believe much in death-bed repentances and spasmodic reforms. We shall neither spread a lie, upon our past conduct, by avouching repentance that we do not feel, nor live a lie now by protestations that would be false. What we have done, we have done — what we have written, we have written.

"We have failed in our cause, and we sit surrounded with the ruins of our former estate."

The *Mercury* published for two more years before shutting down in November

1868. Robert Barnwell Rhett, the father of secession, moved to Louisiana, where he died in 1876. The younger Rhett followed, settling in New Orleans. He continued in the newspaper business, was active in the Democratic Party and worked tirelessly to rehabilitate his father's image – and to continue his attacks on Jefferson Davis, his father's longtime nemesis.

Charleston never regained the prominence it held in the antebellum United States. Reconstruction was a difficult period, the city slow to recover from the ravages of war and the collapse of the slave industry. In 1886 an earthquake nearly leveled the city followed seven years later by a hurricane that devastated much of the Lowcountry. Charleston would eventually rise from the ashes, but it took decades. After 150 years, the old times have yet to be forgotten.

NOTES

S ourcing a narrative newspaper article can be a clumsy endeavor. There are no footnotes or endnotes to keep the story clear of these speed bumps; you just have to live with them, even though they break the spell of storytelling. For the newspaper series that begat this book, sourcing was kept at a minimum because most of the material came from a single resource: the Charleston *Mercury*. When we started on this project, editor Rick Nelson and I chose to base it on the *Mercury* because it was a great hook, but also because there was not nearly enough time to wade through 150 years of Civil War scholarship. A happy byproduct of that format was that it cut down on attribution, or made it part of the story. The newspaper, and certainly editor Robert Barnwell Rhett Jr., became not only characters, but narrators.

When expanding the series to book length – it is half-again as long as *The Post and Courier* series – I once again relied heavily on the reportage of the Charleston *Mercury*. A lot of the new material here is from the paper, and could be classified as details left out of the original serial for space considerations. But this format offers the luxury of stretching out, expanding the reach and perspective. And with endnotes, there is no need to break the spell of the storytelling. These endnotes don't list specifics issues of the *Mercury* that were used, but offer a guide, and credit, to the other sources that make this a richer narrative of Charleston at war.

Chapter 1: Mercury Rising

15 *Rhett was born*: Much of the biographical information on Robert Barnwell Rhett was gleaned from William C. Davis' *Rhett: The Turbulent Life and Times of a Fire-Eater*. Columbia, S.C.: University of South Carolina Press, 2001.

16 *Rhett found a*: The test oath anecdote is largely recounted using William H.

and Jane H. Pease's *James Louis Petigru: Southern Conservative, Southern Dissenter.* Athens, Ga.: University of Georgia Press, 1995, 52-67.

17 *In 1857, Rhett*: Davis, Rhett, 354-374.

18 *South Carolina held*: Information on the statistics of the slave trade in the state, and Charleston in particular, was provided by the Old Slave Mart Museum. Thanks to Nichole Green, director. Michael Allen of the National Park Service also provided a number of key details.

19 *The Southerners demanded*: Edgar, Walter. *South Carolina: A History.* Columbia, S.C.: University of South Carolina Press, 1998, 349.

20 *Doubleday had never*: The Union view of Charleston is largely informed by Abner Doubleday's *Reminiscences of Forts Sumter and Moultrie in 1860-61.* Charleston: Nautical & Aviation Publishing Company of North America, 1998 (reprint), 25-28.

Chapter 2: 'The Union is Dissolved'

26 *Days earlier, when*: Pease, *James Louis Petigru*, 156.

27 *Mary Boykin Chestnut*: Ibid.

29 *Williams Middleton, owner*: The information about the Middleton family, their plantations and the slaves on their properties, was graciously supplied by M. Tracey Todd, director of museums at Middleton Place Foundation.

Chapter 3: Acts of War

35 *Soon after the*: Doubleday, *Reminiscences of Forts Sumter and Moultrie in 1860-61*, 56-57.

35 *As the rumors*: Ibid, 48-49.

37 *Until the last*: This account of Maj. Anderson's last night at Fort Moultrie is reconstructed in part with Doubleday, *Reminiscences of Forts Sumter and Moultrie in 1860-61*, 61-67.

Chapter 4: The Best Laid Plans

49 *The day before*: Doubleday, *Reminiscences of Forts Sumter and Moultrie in 1860-61*, 100.

51 *On Jan. 21*: Part of the story of the South Carolina flag's origin came from the *Mercury*, but many details are courtesy of Wylma Anne Wates, *A Flag Worthy of Your*

State and People: The History of the South Carolina State Flag. Columbia: Department of Archives and History, 1996.

52 *But Rhett was*: Davis, *Rhett*, 423-425.

Chapter 5: Fort Sumter

56 *Gov. Francis Pickens*: Doubleday, *Reminiscences of Forts Sumter and Moultrie in 1860-61*, 113-114.

58 *Mary Boykin Chesnut*: This insight, and several other gems sprinkled throughout the early chapters, come from one of the first classics of Civil War literature, *Mary Boykin Chesnut, A Diary From Dixie.* Boston: Houghton Mifflin, 1949 (reprint), 33.

59 *A ship was*: Ibid, 32.

59 *The R.H. Shannon*: Doubleday, *Reminiscences of Forts Sumter and Moultrie in 1860-61*, 135-136.

60 *Things are happening*: Chesnut, *A Diary From Dixie*, 35.

61 *Mary Chesnut reported*: Ibid, 36.

62 *Later, some would*: Doubleday, *Reminiscences of Forts Sumter and Moultrie in 1860-61*, 143.

62 *I sprang out*: Chesnut, *A Diary From Dixie*, 36.

62 *Inside Fort Sumter*: The behind-the-scenes look at the fort during the bombardment comes largely from Doubleday, *Reminiscences of Forts Sumter and Moultrie in 1860-61*, 143-174.

62 *Anderson wanted to*: These details, and several others in this chapter, were provided by National Park Service historian Richard W. Hatcher III – an unmatched wealth of information on Fort Sumter and all things Civil War.

65 *Despite the barrage*: Doubleday, *Reminiscences of Forts Sumter and Moultrie in 1860-61*, 148.

67 *One excited soldier*: This anecdote was told by historian Richard W. Hatcher III at a re-enactment of the Fort Sumter surrender on the 150th anniversary of the event, April 14, 2011.

Chapter 6: Dixie Land

70 *For readers unimpressed*: These new and improvised lyrics to "Dixie Land," printed in the *Mercury* on May 27, 1861, are a great bit of local color – and a prime

example of just how tightly written the original newspaper serial had to be to fit into *The Post and Courier*.

Chapter 7: Battle Royal

79 *Edward Middleton, younger*: The letters of Edward Middleton, which so perfectly illustrate the brother vs. brother aspect of the Civil War, were provided by M. Tracey Todd, director of museums at Middleton Place Foundation.

80 *Flag Officer Samuel*: Some additional details of the attack on Port Royal were taken from Arthur M. Wilcox and Warren Ripley's *The Civil War at Charleston*, Charleston: Evening Post Publishing, 1966, 23-26.

Chapter 8: Fire

87 *In later years*: The notes of Moses Henry Nathan, Charleston's fire chief in 1861, add a number of details to the account of the Great Fire. That information, as well as several other telling anecdotes, is culled from Marie Ferrara, "Moses Henry Nathan and the Great Charleston Fire of 1861," *The South Carolina Historical Magazine*, vol. 104, no. 4, October 2003, 258-280. Thanks to Harlan Greene and Marie Ferrara of the Special Collections Department at the College of Charleston's Marlen and Nathan Addlestone Library.

Chapter 9: Troubled Waters

101 *Inspired by similar*: June Murray Wells, director of the United Daughters of the Confederacy's Confederate Museum in downtown Charleston, provided information about the ladies' campaign to build the *Palmetto State*. She provided a great article as well, Marguerite Couturier Steedman, "The Ladies Build a Gunboat," *Sandlapper*, September 1968.

Chapter 10: The Straw Hat Ruse

104 *Then the Yankees*: The information on the shelling of Fort Pulaski was provided by the National Park Service.

105 *Most men signed*: Information provided by June Murray Wells, director of the United Daughters of the Confederacy's Confederate Museum on the Market in downtown Charleston. The museum is housed in the very room mentioned in this

passage, and it looks much the same as it did then – except for all the memorabilia. That came later, when the men who fought in the war brought all their souvenirs back to the room where their journey began. A museum was born.

107 *Robert Smalls had*: Additional biographical information, and details of his daring escape from Charleston, was provided by the Robert Smalls Foundation. More information is available at www.robertsmalls.org.

Chapter 11: Secessionville

115 *Neither Confederate nor*: E. Milby Burton, *The Siege of Charleston, 1861-1865*, Columbia: University of South Carolina Press, 1970, 98-99. Burton's classic provides several key details to the battle of Secessionville throughout this chapter.

119 *But not before*: Important details about the first stage of the battle were supplied by Randy Burbage, a past president of the South Carolina Sons of Confederate Veterans, a founding member of the state Hunley Commission and a guy who has probably forgotten more about this war than most people will ever know. Also, he is a descendent of Julius A. Shuler, the fallen member of the 1st S.C. Artillery mentioned in this passage.

121 *You will not*: Burton, *The Siege of Charleston 1861-1865*, 110.

121 *Where could we*: Ibid, 110.

Chapter 12: The Palmetto State

123 *These women sold*: Many details from this opening scene are from the *Mercury,* but other details were taken from Steedman, "The Ladies Build a Gunboat" in *Sandlapper,* September 1968.

126 *Two war-related deaths*: Ibid; Davis, *Rhett*, 512.

130 *The Mercedita had*: Information about the *Mercedita* and several other blockade ships was provided by the Naval Historical Center. For more information about this ships, visit the NHC at www.history.navy.mil.

Chapter 13: Invasion Imminent

139 *Confederate military leaders were*: The April 1863 attack on Fort Sumter has been expanded from its original newspaper length, largely by including additional reportage from the *Mercury.* However, it has been supplemented here by Burton, *The*

Siege of Charleston 1861-1865, 132-142.

142 *Union Brig. Gen.*: Ibid, 140-141.

Chapter 14: Morris Island

146 *For the next*: Burton, *The Siege of Charleston 1861-1865*, 159-160. Burton's account of the battle illustrates just how comprehensive the *Mercury*'s coverage of the Battle of Morris Island actually was. There are few details in Burton's excellent recount of this engagement that are not found in Rhett's newspaper. This, however, is one of them.

149 *Gen. Gillmore had*: Ibid, 162-164.

150 *Men fell by*: Ibid, 166.

Chapter 15: The Siege

159 *The shells all*: While the *Mercury* provided what few details survive about that first night of the siege, Burton, *The Siege of Charleston 1861-1865*, 254-258, provides additional detail here.

Chapter 16: Sumter Strikes Back

166 *A New Orleans*: The additional details on the early history of the *H.L. Hunley* are taken from Brian Hicks and Schuyler Kropf's *Raising the Hunley: The Remarkable History and Recovery of the Lost Confederate Submarine*. New York: Ballantine, 2002, 36-45.

169 *One Georgia soldier*: Burton, *The Siege of Charleston 1861-1865*, 180.

170 *Union Admiral John*: Ibid, 194.

Chapter 17: A Presidential Visit

177 *The submarine had*: Hicks and Kropf, *Raising the Hunley*, 47-51.

Chapter 18: Fish-boat

185 *Gardner Smith, a*: Hicks and Kropf, *Raising the Hunley*, 50-51.

189 *One soldier, Henry*: Information about the extended Middleton family was provided by M. Tracey Todd, director of museums at Middleton Place Foundation.

189 *After the Hunley*: This extended account of the *H.L. Hunley*'s historic mission

uses information largely culled from Hicks and Kropf, *Raising the Hunley*, 53-75.

191 *There is one*: Brian Hicks, "Hunley's Captain Fiercely Determined to Succeed," *The Post and Courier,* April 11, 2004.

Chapter 19: "A future most awful'

200 *That same weekend*: The account of the battle of Bloody Bridge – which is re-enacted at Legare Farms every year as "The Battle of Charleston" – got very little mention in the original newspaper serial. This account is taken from the bare-bones information provided in the *Mercury*, supplemented by Milby Burton's more detailed account in *The Siege of Charleston 1861-1865*, 287-295.

Chapter 20: City of Ruins

212 *It was, historian*: Additional details on the night the Confederates abandoned Charleston is taken from Burton, *The Siege of Charleston 1861-1865*, 316-325; and Wilcox and Ripley, *The Civil War at Charleston*, 76-77.

Epilogue: The Cause, Lost

215 *The truth is*: Burton, *The Siege of Charleston 1861-1865*, 312-313.

215 *The Union sent*: Ibid, 322.

216 *Any one who*: Ibid, 324.

216 *The fall of*: The bulk of this epilogue's description of Charleston following the Union occupation comes from a single source: Charles Carleton Coffin, *The Boys of '61; or, Our Years of Fighting: Personal Observation with the Army and Navy*. Boston: Estes and Lauriat, 1881, 462-489.

ACKNOWLEDGEMENTS

This book could not have been written without 18 months of support, help and encouragement from *Post and Courier* Content Editor Rick Nelson. Rick took on this project at the same time I did and, despite his many duties at the paper, he always had time to serve as sounding board, advisor and editor. If that weren't enough, he also edited this book in manuscript form because no one knew the material better – and there's no one I trust more.

A good number of people at *The Post and Courier* also lent assistance to the original newspaper serial this book is based upon. Many thanks to Bill Hawkins, Tom Clifford, Andy Lyons, Melanie Balog, Betsy Miller, John Kerr, Shirley Greene, Jane Green, Tim Thorsen, Leroy Burnell, Schuyler Kropf, Steve Wagenlander, Ben Morgan, Fred Rindge, Grace Beahm and Becky Baulch.

Photo director Tom Spain spent a lot of time researching the pictures and photos that appeared with the series and in these pages, and his expertise – along with graphic artist Gill Guerry – make this book look great. In the newspaper's library, Libby Wallace and Pam Liles helped me sort through five years of microfilm. And a special nod to Ohio native Bob Kinney, who served as copy editor on the original series – and vowed not to edit it if I changed the ending.

At Evening Post Books, John Burbage deserves a great deal of credit. As publisher and editor, he always had a clear vision of what this book could be and guided it through the process with a deft hand. I appreciate all his work on this project, not the least of which was his astute final edit. John's staff is first-rate as well. And of course, thanks to Pierre Manigault for the chance to do this sort of work.

Around Charleston, a number of people offered invaluable information and guidance as I tried to reconstruct the city's past. June Murray Wells, director of the United

Daughters of the Confederacy's Confederate Museum, always seemed to have just what I needed. My good friend Randy Burbage is a walking encyclopedia of war knowledge and pointed out several vital facts and anecdotes. Richard W. Hatcher III, the National Park Service historian at Fort Sumter, knows more about this area's Civil War history than anyone I know and has been generous with his time and knowledge.

Thanks also to Nichole Green at the Old Slave Mart Museum; Tracey Todd at Middleton Place Foundation; Grahame Long at the Charleston Museum; Michael Coker at the Old Exchange Building and Provost Dungeon; Harlan Greene and Marie Ferrara at the College of Charleston; Anne Cleveland and the staff of the Charleston Library Society; Michael Allen with the National Park Service; Kellen Correia, Raegan Quinn and Josephine Starnes at Friends of the Hunley; and the staff of the Gibbes Museum of Art. Outside of the city, I received a good deal of assistance from Eric Emerson, director of the state Department of Archives and History, Allen Roberson at the Confederate Relic Room and the staff of the Museum of the Confederacy in Richmond.

And, as always, thanks to my family: Beth, Cole and Nate, the only native Charlestonian among us. I also appreciate the help and support of Alan and Donna Spears, and of course Judy Hicks. And finally, a special nod to my good friend Steve Mullins, who suggested this.

CITY OF RUIN

INDEX

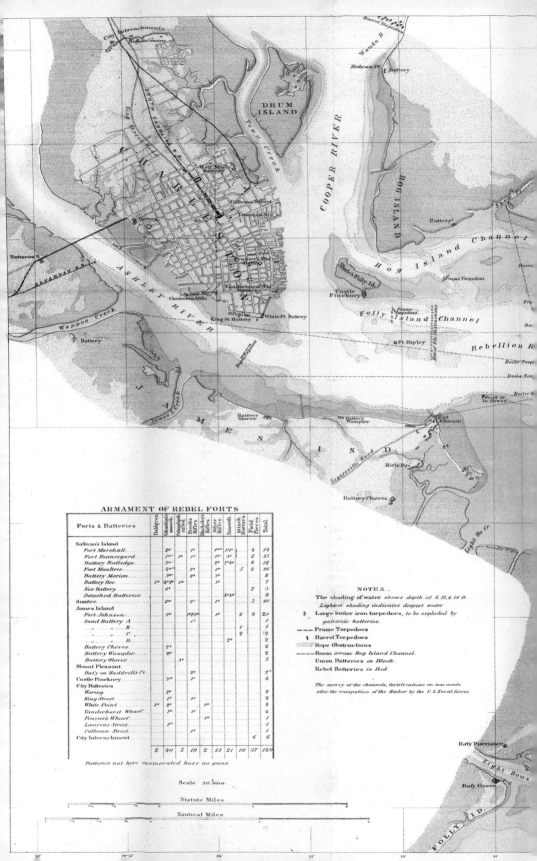

ARMAMENT OF REBEL FORTS

Forts & Batteries	Dahlgren	Columbiads smooth.	Columbiads rifled.	Brooke Rifled.	Blackeleys Rifles	Other Rifles	Smooth.	Island Mortars	Field Pieces	Total.
Sullivan's Island										
Fort Marshall	2ᵘ		1ᵘ		1ᵘᵘ	1⁴ᵘ			4	14
Fort Beauregard	1ᵘᵘ	1ˢ	1ᵘ		1ˢ	3ˢ			2	13
Battery Rutledge	3ᵘᵘ				2ˢ	2⁴ˢ		5	8	12
Fort Moultrie	4ᵘᵘ		2ˢ		1ᵘ		5	2		16
Battery Marion	3ᵘᵘ		4ˢ		3ˢ					8
Battery Bee	1ˢ	4ˢᵖ	1ᵘ		3ˢ				2	7
New Battery	4ˢ									3
Detached Batteries					4ˢ4ˢ					8
Sumter	2ˢᵘ		2ˢ		1ˢ				5	10
James Island										
Fort Johnson	5ᵘᵘ		2ˢ2ᵖ		1ˢ			2	8	20
Sand Battery A			1ˢ					1		1
„ „ B								1		1
„ „ C								2		2
„ „ D						2ˢ				2
Battery Cheves		2ˢ								2
Battery Wampler		2ᵘᵘ								2
Battery Glover			3ˢ							3
Mount Pleasant										
Baty on Haddrells Pt			2ˢ						2ˢ	4
Castle Pinckney		3ˢ	1ˢ							4
City Batteries										
Waring		2ˢ								2
King Street		1ˢ	1ˢ							2
White Point	1ˢ	2ˢ		1ˢ						4
Vanderhorst Wharf		1ᵘᵘ	1ˢ							2
Frazier's Wharf				1ˢ						1
Laurens Street		1ˢ								1
Calhoun Street			1ˢ							1
City Intrenchment									6	6
	2	40	5	19	2	13	21	10	37	149

Batteries not here enumerated have no guns.

Scale 30.000

Statute Miles.

Nautical Miles.

NOTES.

The shading of water shows depth at 6, 12, & 18 ft. Lightest shading indicates deepest water

◖ Large boiler iron torpedoes, to be exploded by galvanic batteries.

━ ━ ━ Frame Torpedoes

♦ Barrel Torpedoes

///// Rope Obstructions

━━━━ Boom across Hog Island Chaanel.

Union Batteries in Black.

Rebel Batteries in Red.

The survey of the channels, fortifications &c. was made after the occupation of the Harbor by the U. S. Naval forces.